WALK INTO PURPOSE

WALK INTO PURPOSE

*52-Week Devotional Journal to
Draw You Closer to God
in Order to Walk in Purpose*

ALESHA DOBOS

WESTBOW
PRESS®
A DIVISION OF THOMAS NELSON
& ZONDERVAN

WestBow Press books may be ordered through booksellers or by contacting:

WestBow Press
A Division of Thomas Nelson & Zondervan
1663 Liberty Drive
Bloomington, IN 47403
www.westbowpress.com
844-714-3454

ISBN: 978-1-6642-7127-2 (sc)
ISBN: 978-1-6642-7129-6 (hc)
ISBN: 978-1-6642-7128-9 (e)

Print information available on the last page.

WestBow Press rev. date: 09/21/2022

To my grandmother,
Jeannette Vernon,
along with my cousin,
Jasmine Marie Traylor

ACKNOWLEDGMENTS

First and foremost, to God. Without You I am nothing. Holy Spirit, as gentle and powerful as You are, I could not have done this without You. All of this is a result of Your trust in me. It is an honor and a privilege to share what I have gained in our secret place with the world.

To my mom, Deborah Patillo. Thank you for your constant support and prayers. Even as an adult, you have been there when I needed you. I have gained the best part of you – your love for God and for people, and your selfless heart of giving.

To my Apostle Yolanda Stith and Pastor Kori Stith. Thank you for your "yes." Because of you, I have received true deliverance, have come into my identity as a daughter, and now I am able to walk in purpose. I was able to birth something beautiful out of wholeness. Thank you for your consistency, integrity, and love. I love you both.

To my best friend, Yemi. Thank you for always being there for me, speaking life into the dead parts of me, and believing in me when I didn't even believe in myself. You have seen every side of me and have stayed by my side and remained consistent for the last 16 years. Thank you for your prayers, correction, wisdom, and love.

To the rest of my family, friends, and church family, thank you! Thank you for your love, prayers, and support. I love you!

CONTENTS

INTRODUCTION

Everyone goes through different stages in their lives. Not one day or week will look the same no matter how structured and organized one tries to be. You may have really great days when you are on fire for God and feel unstoppable. Then you experience moments of sadness or grief. You have days where you are struggling with sin, fear, doubt, or hopelessness. Life's circumstances cause you to feel distant from God. In the mist of warfare and on the verge of giving up, you need encouragement. Maybe you feel as though you are on a rollercoaster with your relationship with God, constantly going up and down. The thing is, God doesn't move; people do. God is always there waiting for an invitation to dine with you. God is always there waiting for you to initiate your time with Him. He longs to speak to you. He longs to share His heart with you. He longs for intimacy with you. He longs for you to know Him as Abba Father. He longs for you to come into your full identity as His son or daughter. He longs for you to walk in purpose and to be all He created and called you to be. The enemy comes to kill, steal, and destroy. It is his goal to separate you from the Father by causing you to question your identity and the Father's love for you. However, it is up to you to cast down the lies of the enemy, shift your mindset, fight for your identity daily (because you do not wrestle against flesh and blood), and be consistent in your pursuit of intimacy with the Father. This will enable you to walk in your purpose.

Walk into Purpose can either be completed in chronological order or any order based on your need, situation, or season. It can be completed individually, with your family or friends, or as a small group in college or at church. This devotional is meant to challenge you, encourage you, and grow you spiritually, mentally, and emotionally. It is my goal to encourage you to persevere through the hardships, warfare, and trials and tribulations so that you can remain consistent with your pursuit of intimacy with the Father and be all that God called you to be. Without knowing God as Abba and coming into your identity as His son or daughter, you cannot walk in the fullness of your purpose. It is my hope that this 52-week interactive devotional will draw you closer to God, help you come into your identity, and push you to walk in your purpose. Each devotional includes weekly prayers, declarations, and/or spaces for reflection.

Disclaimer: Walk into Purpose is not to be used to replace the Bible but to encourage you to go deeper in the Word, learn more about who God is, strengthen your relationship with Him as Abba, and discover your "why" so you can be all that God created you to be.

Week 1

TRUST GOD'S TIMING

He replied, "The Father alone has the authority to set those
dates and times, and they are not for you to know."
~~Acts 1:7 NLT~~

So many times we ask God, "when is this going to happen?" or "when is that going to happen?" In this passage, the disciples wanted to know when Jesus was going to restore Israel. And like them, we are reminded that His timing is perfect, to trust Him, and to have faith that He has not forgotten about us.

You may be looking at your age and wondering when you are going to get married. You see your family and friends being successful while you're living paycheck to paycheck. What about your purpose? You know God has called you to do great things, but you're not living it out. In your frustration, you ask, "Lord, when is it going to be my turn?!"

The Lord told Jeremiah, "Before I formed you in the womb I knew you; Before you were born I sanctified you; I ordained you a prophet to the nations" (Jeremiah 1:5 NKJV). God may not have called you to be a prophet, but you were called to do something great. You were born with a purpose. Be encouraged! Like Jeremiah, before you were born, God had a plan for you. He knew exactly what you were going to do and when you were going to do it. If God can feed the birds and clothe the lilies, how much more does He care about you (Matthew 6:25-30)?

You see, God doesn't want you to feel like you don't have a purpose because you do. He doesn't want you to struggle because He desires for you to live a prosperous life. He doesn't want you to feel lonely because He desires an intimate relationship with you. However, you have to do your part too. Matthew 6:33 (NLT) says, "Seek the Kingdom of God above all else, and live righteously, and he will give you everything you need."

Trust His plan. Trust the process. Trust His timing. Do not worry about things you have no control over. You're so busy looking at other people's lives instead of discovering who you are in Christ and who He created you to be. Your path is not like anyone else's on this earth. You are right where you need to be. Don't spend time worrying about where you are in life or what you don't have. Instead, have faith and trust God to bring your purpose into full circle. You are not fulfilled because you haven't discovered your purpose yet. Pursue God as Abba, pursue sonship, and pursue purpose. Everything else will fall in place.

REFLECTION

This week's prayer:
Lord, I surrender my doubts, fears, and worries to You. Forgive me for wanting to go outside of Your timing. Help me to trust the plans You have for my life. You know what is best for me. I surrender to the process. Guide me with wisdom and knowledge of the Holy Spirit in every area of my life. Father, You will not misguide me or lead me astray. I thank You because You will work everything out for my good. I have nothing to worry about because You are in control. I will not lean on my own understanding, but instead, I will trust You with all of my heart and acknowledge You in everything that I do. In Jesus' name, amen.

God wants you to trust Him with your whole heart. What areas in your life are you currently struggling to trust God in?

_____

_____

_____

_____

_____

_____

_____

What are some things you can to do this week that will give you the freedom to completely surrender and trust God? Return at the end of the week to document your progress.

_____

_____

_____

_____

_____

_____

_____

Week 2

OVERCOMING WEAPONS OF THE ENEMY

"No weapon formed against you shall prosper, and every tongue *which*
rises against you in judgment you shall condemn. This *is* the heritage of the
servants of the Lord, and their righteousness *is* from Me," says the Lord.
~~Isaiah 54:17 NKJV ~~

Everyone goes through hard times in life, and one of the key scriptures to keep in mind is Isaiah 54:17. As a Christian, you can be a target to the enemy at any given moment. These attacks can come from family, friends or enemies, while at work, at school, or even while running errands. Why? Because the power of darkness is working against you. Ephesians 6:12 (NKJV) says, "For we do not wrestle against flesh and blood, but against principalities, against powers, against the rulers of darkness of this age, against spiritual hosts of wickedness in heavenly places." The enemy will try to use any technique to get you to fall short of God's glory, to discourage you, and to make you give up. However, there is a solution. God has given you the equipment you need to fight back. You have access to the full armor of God! Ephesians 6:14-18 instructs you to *put on* the belt of truth, the breastplate of righteousness, the shoes of peace, the helmet of salvation, and the sword of the Spirit (which is the Word of God). You also have to pray in the Spirit with supplication. Prayer is a weapon. In doing this (putting on and applying the armor of God and praying), the tactics of the enemy cannot work. Anything he tries to throw at you will not prosper, and every accusatory tongue that rises against you will be exposed and dismantled. You are more than a conqueror; you are victorious!

Another thing you can do is meditate on the Word of God. When the Bible tells you to meditate on the Word night and day (Joshua 1:8), that means to read, study, and apply. It means to memorize it and have it in your arsenal so you can pull it out and pray over the Word whenever you need encouragement, hope, peace, faith, joy, protection, provision, and anything else you may need from the Lord. Meditating on the Word could also mean saying a quick prayer, quoting scriptures in your head, reading devotionals, or journaling throughout the day. You do not have to spend hours in a secluded place. You can be in your car, office, bathroom, kitchen, at the park, or in the store. God is with you everywhere you go and hears everything you say. He will never leave you or forsake you (Deuteronomy 31:6). Meditating on the Word of God night and day allows you to connect with God while staying alert and reminding you to always put Him first. This also lets Satan know that whatever plan he has for your life will not follow through because you are focused on God.

God is your Rock and firm foundation. From the beginning of time, He has been consistent, ever-present, and never changing. He is stable in all of His ways. He does not slumber nor will He allow your foot to be moved (Psalms 121:3). He is your Protector and Refuge in times of trouble. No matter what Satan throws at you (hatred, peer pressure, lust, drugs, envy, confusion, idolatry, division, etc.), you have to find strength in the Holy Spirit to say no to your flesh. You have to use your God-given authority to resist the enemy so he can flee (James 4:7). It is time for you put on the full armor of God, and fight! You are an overcomer, and you will win!

REFLECTION

Military soldiers are constantly on guard when they are in the midst of a warzone. They are always watching and listening for anything that could lead to an attack from the enemy. Like a soldier, stay alert and be on guard this week. Every morning, put on the full armor of God (Ephesians 6:13-18). Remind yourself that you are not fighting against flesh and blood but against principalities and spiritual wickedness. You never know when the enemy is going to attack so you have to be ready and on guard.

This week's prayer:
Lord, You know what today is going to bring. You can see things in the spirit realm that I cannot see. Send angels to surround me and fight on my behalf. Give me the wisdom and discernment I need to defend myself and attack the enemy properly. Help me to respond in a godly manner and allow my first response to be a godly response. If things are out of my control, remind me that You will not allow my foot to be moved. Although I have the full armor of God, I also know that You are my great Defender. You fight my battles and vengeance belongs to You. Holy Spirit, I ask that You guide me. I submit my thoughts and my emotions into Your hands. In Jesus' name, amen.

This week's declaration:
No weapon formed against me shall prosper. I am wearing the full armor of God. I have on the helmet of salvation, the breastplate of righteousness, the shield of faith, the shoes of peace, the belt of truth, and the sword of the Spirit! Satan is defeated and I am an overcomer!

Throughout the week, reflect on these things:

1. How has the enemy tried to attack you this week, if at all?

_____

_____

_____

_____

_____

_____

_____

_____

_____

_____

_____

_____

2. How did you handle the situation? Did you allow the enemy to get the best of you? If so, what could you have done differently?

_____

_____

_____

_____

_____

_____

_____

_____

_____

_____

_____

_____

Week 3

GOD'S VINEYARD

*In that day, sing about the fruitful vineyard. I, the Lord, will watch over it,
watering it carefully. Day and night I will watch so no one can harm it.*
~~Isaiah 27:2-3 NLT~~

In this passage, *vineyard* is referring to the church (body of Christ). Another
reference can be found in Isaiah 5:1-7. In the natural, a vineyard is property that
belongs to or is owned by a particular individual (vigneron). Vineyards are used to
produce the choicest wines. To do that, a vineyard must be watched over, watered,
and attended to daily to ensure the safety and development of the grapes.

Like a vigneron watches over and cares for their vineyard, so does God with you.
God watches over you (protects and defends), waters you (provides), and attends
to you (takes care of). God is the great I AM. Everything you need Him to be, He
is. As His child, He provides for your every need and watches over you so that
no one can harm you. Day and night, He does this so that you can grow, mature,
become fruitful, and be chosen to do the work of the Kingdom. You are set apart
like grapes in a vineyard. Not every grape is chosen to go through the process of
producing the choicest wine. "For many are called, but few are chosen" (Matthew
22:14 NKJV). God called you to be a "chosen people, a royal priesthood, a holy
nation, God's special possession, that you may declare the praises of him who
called you out of darkness into his wonderful light" (1 Peter 2:9 NIV).

Grapes do not just turn into wine by squeezing all the juice out; they have to
go through a process. Grapes have to be crushed, de-stemmed, fermented, and
pressed again to get the last bit of the remaining juice out. Like grapes, you have
to go through a process that doesn't always feel good in the moment but will be
worth it in the end. The crushing humbles you; it brings you to your knees and
causes you to surrender. De-stemming allows God to remove everything that is
not like Him out of your life. Fermentation develops your character and makes
you more like Him. And when it seems as though you've made it… when it seems
like you finally have it all together, you are crushed, tested, and tried again so you
can come out purified, holy, and ready to be used by God.

Isn't it amazing how God calls you His vineyard? To a vigneron, a vineyard is their
special possession and something they deeply cherish that can produce something so
rich and of great value. When those grapes go through their process and finally turn
into wine, they take pride in what they have created. Wow! That is how God sees you.

REFLECTION

Wherever you are in life with your process – whether you are in a crushing season, being de-stemmed, being fermented, or at the final crushing phase – take joy in it because you are going to come out humbled, purified, and ready to be used by God. You are going to come out secure in your identity with a clear understanding of who God created you to be, and you are going to take the world by storm!

Use the space below to reflect on where you are in your process. What are you going through? What challenges are you facing? How does it make you feel? What lesson is God trying to teach you? What area in your life is He trying to stretch or grow you in? What are some potential positive outcomes? How can you respond differently? These questions are important because they will help you see your situation differently and shift your focus back to God.

_____

_____

_____

_____

_____

_____

_____

_____

_____

_____

_____

_____

_____

_____

_____

_____

_____

_____

_____

_____

Week 4

DINING WITH GOD

Behold, I stand at the door and knock. If anyone hears My voice and opens
the door, I will come in to him and dine with him, and him with Me.
~~Revelation 3:20 NKJV~~

Let's break down this scripture.

I stand: This is in present tense. God is continuously standing, never resting, in the moment, at this present time, in this instant, always and forever until the end of time.

At the door: God is standing at the door of people's hearts.

And knock: God is waiting for entrance or admittance.

If anyone hears My voice: God's Word and Spirit.

And opens the door: Welcome God in and willingly receive Him as Savior and Father.

I will come in to him: However you are, whatever circumstances you're in, or how much you have sinned, God will come in and purify your heart and spirit.

And dine with him: God will commune with you while refreshing your spirit and renewing your mind so you can walk in the fullness and power of the Holy Spirit.

And him with Me: As God dines with you and you with Him, intimacy and connection take place between you and God. It's a great exchange! Because of your willingness to let Him in, you can bond with God in a way that is personal and intimate. Your willingness to dine with God on earth also grants you the favor of dining with Him in eternity.

You cannot dine with God if you do not let Him in. When you go out to eat with a friend, that moment is special and intimate. You are not worrying about life or what is going on around you. You are giving and receiving from each other with undivided attention. You are catching up, laughing, and listening intently to one another. After the meal, there is a greater appreciation, a deeper connection, a stronger bond, and a deeper love. That is what God desires from you. Will you let Him in?

REFLECTION

God is always at the door. When He knocks and calls out to you this week, open the door and let Him in. I want to challenge you this week to find a quiet spot and have a conversation with Jesus. You can even go to a café, bring your bible and a notebook, and journal your conversation. You're not praying or asking for things, but just enjoying each other's presence. Get to know His heart. Ask Him how His day is going. Ask Him what put a smile on His face today. Ask Him what burdens His heart. Talk to Him and wait for Him to respond. Maybe He will show you a vision or speak to your spirit. If you are good at drawing, perhaps He will speak to you through your art. If you have never done it before, it may feel weird at first, but as you make time for the Lord and press into His presence, He will respond. Don't give up or get discouraged. Keep pressing and waiting. The Lord is looking for a willing heart.

At the end of the week, share one of your favorite moments with God during your quiet, intimate time with Him.

_____

_____

_____

_____

_____

_____

_____

_____

_____

_____

_____

_____

_____

_____

_____

_____

_____

Week 5

RECEIVING POWER

But you will receive power when the Holy Spirit comes upon you. And
you will be my witnesses, telling people about me everywhere—in
Jerusalem, throughout Judea, in Samaria, and to the ends of the earth.
~~Acts 1:8 NLT~~

Power is translated from the Greek word, *dynamis* or *dunamis*. It means:

1. Inherent power, power residing in a thing by virtue of its nature, or which a person or thing exerts and puts forth.
2. Power for performing miracles.
3. Moral power and excellence of soul.
4. The power and influence which belong to riches and wealth.
5. Power and resources arising from numbers.
6. Power consisting in or resting upon armies, forces, hosts. [1]

When you receive the gift of the Holy Spirit and Holy Spirit comes upon you, you receive *dunamis* power. What does that mean for you? Your body is the temple of the Holy Spirit (1 Corinthians 6:19), meaning Holy Spirit lives and dwells within you. You have inherent power that exists or resides in you permanently. You have the power to perform miracles. You have power and influence that belongs to riches and wealth. You have power of resources arising from numbers, meaning you have access to an abundance of resources because your Father owns the cattle on a thousand hills (Psalms 50:10). If God told you to do something, He will supply you with the resources you need to complete it. You also have power to fight off the enemy. Ephesians 6:11 (NLT) tells you to put on the full armor of God so that you can stand firm against the enemy's strategies. You win wars by praying, fasting, declaring the Word of God, and resisting the devil.

So why don't enough people operate in dunamis power? Some people don't believe they have that type of power to actually walk in it. Others may have a small measure of faith (Romans 12:3). We know that faith without works is dead (James 2:17), which is saying faith is an action that must be put to work so that it can develop. The more you put your faith to work, the more it will grow.

Start believing, declaring, and walking in the dunamis power that is in you. Power and might are in your hands. Use it to enhance the Kingdom, to do the work of the Lord, to bring people to Christ, and to operate in the gifts God has given you. Power is in your DNA. It is who you are! Be guided by the Holy Spirit and don't be afraid to use it.

REFLECTION

In what ways have you used dunamis power this week?

Day 1:

_____

_____

_____

Day 2:

_____

_____

_____

Day 3:

_____

_____

_____

Day 4:

_____

_____

_____

Day 5:

_____

_____

_____

Day 6:

_____

_____

_____

Day 7:

_____

_____

_____

Week 6

GOD IS ABLE

Now to Him who is able to do exceedingly abundantly above all
that we ask or think, according to the power that works in us.
~~Ephesians 3:20 NKJV~~

According to Proverbs 18:21, there is power in the tongue, and what you speak can come to past. But in Ephesians 3:20, the Bible says God is able to do exceedingly abundantly above all that you ask or *think*. Imagine what God could do just by you *thinking* it before you even speak it! Something profound happens when you think – you picture it in your mind. Seeing is believing, even if it hasn't happened yet. That's faith! "Now faith is the substance of things hoped for, the evidence of things not seen" (Hebrews 11:1 NKJV). If you have enough faith to see it happen before it manifests, God can surely do it!

But there is a condition: according to the power (*dunamis*) that works within you! How do you get that power to work within you? If you look up the Greek word for "work," it translates to *energeō*, which means, to be operative, be at work, put forth power; to work for one, aid one; to effect; to display one's activity, show one's self operative." [2]

What does that mean for you? It means that you have to be active, be operative, be effective, but most importantly, prepare for battle. Why? Because whenever the enemy finds out about a plan that God has for you or sees you enhancing the Kingdom or that you are prospering or sees that you're pursuing purpose, he is going to do everything in his power to try to stop you. You prepare with fasting and praying and trusting in God. Then you actively pursue it. Faith without works is dead (James 2:17). God is not going to just drop purpose in your lap. That book is not going to write itself. That job is not going to appear out of thin air. You have to apply for that position or network. The keys to the house you want is not just going to appear in your hand. You have to save money, increase your credit score, determine where you want to live, and talk to a realtor. You have to be proactive. You have to be effective. You have to be operative. You have to put in the work! God has given you everything you need – provision, resources, talents, and skills to have all of your needs met and to pursue purpose. By doing this, you are working according to the power that is within you ... to see God do exceedingly abundantly above *all* that you ask or think!

REFLECTION

How can you use the power that works within you to make something happen? In other words, what are some steps you can take towards your purpose or goal? Remember, God created you and placed desires in your heart. The only thing is, He is not going to just drop it in your lap. He has already given you everything you need to make it happen. Analyze what God has already put in your life (friends, coworkers, social media, talents, skills, and resources), and utilize it. Apply for that job you don't qualify for. Apply to the school you don't think you will get into. Talk to local business owners and contractors. It's time to start working towards your goals and pursue purpose. Don't put limits on a limitless God! He can do exceedingly and abundantly above all that you ask or think. However, faith without works is *dead*! I don't care if you're reading this in January or July or November; Don't wait until next year. Start now!

What is the one thing you want God to do in your life, or what is one goal you want to achieve? Write the vision and make it plain!

_____

_____

_____

_____

_____

_____

_____

_____

What are some steps you can take to make it happen?

_____

_____

_____

_____

_____

_____

_____

_____

Week 7

EXAMINE YOUR WAYS

Let us carefully examine our ways, and let us return to the Lord.
~~Lamentations 3:40 NET~~

Put yourselves to the test to see if you are in the faith; examine
yourselves! Or do you not recognize regarding yourselves that
Jesus Christ is in you – unless, indeed, you fail the test!
~~2 Corinthians 13:5 NET~~

As a Christian, it is important to examine your walk with God regularly. Doing this causes you to reevaluate yourself and your relationship with the Father. How often do you sit and think, what are some things that I have been struggling with lately? What are some of my soul issues? Am I still struggling with the same sins? Have I picked up another sin? Have I decreased my time with the Lord? How is my relationship with Him? Where do I want my relationship with God to be? What do I need to do to grow deeper in my relationship with God?

We get so busy with our lives that we hardly ask ourselves these questions. There are numerous sins, whether physical, external, or internal. Sometimes, we get comfortable and think we're doing okay, when in reality, there are deeper issues that God wants to deal with. Take a moment to meditate on these questions: Do I love/like God in this moment? Did I allow the frustrations of life to cause resentment towards God and hinder my relationship with Him? In what ways am I showing my love to God and to the world around me?

Think about it this way: most jobs have annual evaluations. Based on that evaluation, you are either going to get promoted, demoted, or fired. You don't want your sin to cause you to get demoted. You also don't get promoted by staying the same because you're doing just enough to get by. Imagine being stuck. You're not growing. There's no desire to spend time with the Lord and your relationship with God has become stagnant. A personal evaluation is necessary so you can work on improving those areas in your life that will draw you closer to God.

It doesn't matter how anointed you are, what your title is, or what ministry you serve on. No one is perfect. Because you are still in this flesh, you will always struggle with things. Without imperfections, there would be no need for grace, redemption, forgiveness, and a Savior. It's important to ask God to reveal those things in your life that are not pleasing to Him. Ask God to open your eyes to see the ugly truth about yourself. It's time to expose and uproot!

REFLECTION

It's time to evaluate yourself. Before going into this, take time to pray. This is not to condemn you but to bring conviction and help you grow.

This week's prayer:
Lord, I humble myself before You. Show me how I have disappointed You recently. Show me areas in my life that You want me to work on. Letting go will not be easy and I will not be able to do this without You. You are the Potter and I am the clay. I am willing to let You begin the work in me. Holy Spirit, bring conviction whenever I do something that does not please You. I want to be more like You. Jesus, I love You and I want a more intimate relationship with You. I want to fellowship with You on a deeper level. Re-spark the intimacy and the fire in our relationship. You are the most important person in my life. In Jesus' name, amen.

I am currently struggling with:

_____

_____

_____

Things I am willing to work on, let go of, or change in this area of my life:

_____

_____

_____

In what ways have I shown my love to God recently?

_____

_____

_____

At the end of the week, examine yourself: My intimacy, relationship, and fellowship with the Lord has increased or changed in this way:

_____

_____

_____

Week 8

TROUBLES OF GREAT JOY

Dear brothers and sisters, when troubles of any kind come your way, consider
it an opportunity for great joy. For you know that when your faith is tested,
your endurance has a chance to grow. So let it grow, for when your endurance
is fully developed, you will be perfect and complete, needing nothing.
~~James 1:2-4 NLT~~

Trouble comes in many different forms. No matter how big or small your problems
are, it still causes you trouble in some way. However, scripture gives you hope.
James said when troubles of *any kind* come your way, consider it an opportunity
for great joy.

Why should you have joy in pain, suffering, persecution, challenges, and
disappointments? Why should you find happiness in those things? Why rejoice,
smile, and praise during hard times? Because you shouldn't look at them as a form
of punishment, as a curse, rejection, or failure. As a son or daughter of God, He
will not purposely do anything to you that will harm or hurt you. His intentions
are not to make your life miserable. Jeremiah 29:11 (NLT) says, "For I know the
plans I have for you," says the Lord. "They are plans for good and not for disaster,
to give you a future and a hope." God only wants the best for you. You can rejoice
and praise God in the mist of your situation knowing that it is only temporary.

When trouble comes your way, put on the belt of truth. What does the Bible say
about your situation? Guard your heart with the breastplate of righteousness.
Walk in peace because your feet are strapped in it. Align your thoughts with the
Word by putting on the helmet of salvation and casting out all false imagination
(2 Corinthians 10:5) pertaining to your situation. Don't become weary and sad.
Don't walk around with your face all pitiful for attention. You have power within
you to change your situation. You have the power of prayer and declaration. Speak
over and praise through your situation until it changes.

When trouble comes your way, your faith is being tested. However, when you
endure, the end result will be victorious. When you overcome temptation or
life's obstacles, you grow because you didn't give up, back down, or fall into the
trap of the enemy. As you conquer sin and the troubles of life, you become more
spiritually mature. There is hope and joy in the mist of your situation. Victory is
waiting for you at the end of your troubles!

REFLECTION

This week's declaration:
I am an overcomer. I will endure to the end. The joy of the Lord is my strength.
I will consider trouble of any kind, great joy. I will not allow confusion into my
life. I will not allow my thoughts to be distorted. I will not allow the enemy to
influence my character or my behavior. I am the child of the Most High God and
I win!

As you are going through this week, write testimonies of how you endured or
overcame your troubles. When your faith is tested, your endurance grows, and
when your endurance grows, it has a chance to fully develop, and when it fully
develops, you become complete, needing nothing. That is a testimony in itself!

1.

_____

_____

_____

_____

2.

_____

_____

_____

_____

3.

_____

_____

_____

_____

Week 9

PRAYING FOR YOUR ENEMIES

However, I say to you, love your enemy, bless the one who curses
you, do something wonderful for the one who hates you, and respond
to the very ones who persecute you by praying for them.
~~Matthew 5:44 TPT~~

Jesus instructs us to love, bless and pray for our enemies. It is not easy to think well of the people who hate, dislike, and mistreat you, let alone do something wonderful for them and pray for them. People like this are often associated with pain, tears, trauma, and/or abuse.

So why does Jesus want you to love, pray, and show kindness to people who don't want anything to do with you? In the following verse (5:45), Jesus tells you that it will reveal your true identity as a child of God. How? Because God is love. When you love like He does, you are being a reflection of Him. You may think, "how can God love this person? Doesn't He know how this person treats me?" Of course He does! But He also sees their trauma, self-hate, low self-esteem, depression, abuse, identity crisis, and jealousy. He also sees their separation from Him. First John 4:18-19 (NLT) says, "Such love has no fear, because perfect love expels all fear. If we are afraid, it is for fear of punishment, and this shows that we have not fully experienced his perfect love. We love each other because he loved us first."

Loving your enemy doesn't mean constantly smiling in their face or hugging them. It means being cordial and polite when you see them. It means not rolling your eyes behind their back when they walk away. It means not returning evil for evil but responding in a godly manner when they respond otherwise. Being consistent in how you show love towards others not only reflects the love of the Father, but it also breaks down their walls and allows them to let their guard down.

You may not see a change right away, and things may seem to get worse before they get better, but you must trust that God is answering your prayers and changing the hearts of your enemies. Praying for them like you would pray for yourself gives you a heart of flesh towards them. It gives you compassion and understanding. It opens your eyes to see them the way God does. Your prayers don't just change them, but it changes you. It may not be easy at first and you may have to pray for strength, patience, and grace as you do, but the end result will be worth it.

Loving your enemies through the process allows you to be receptive to the change when it happens. What do I mean? It prevents you from treating them like the person they used to be because you have been extending love and grace to them the entire time. Think about Apostle Paul. After Saul had his encounter with Jesus in Acts 9, he started going by his dual name, Paul. I can imagine when people heard the name Saul, it was a reminder of who he used to be – the person who hated God and persecuted believers of Christ. But when they heard "Apostle Paul," they were no longer afraid. When they heard the name Paul, they thought about the person who spoke boldly about the Messiah, the one who was persecuted for the sake of the Gospel, and the one who performed miracles.

Your enemy could have a Saul into Paul encounter with God overnight and be completely transformed. However, because of how they treated you, you still remember and treat them like "Saul." It becomes easier to embrace their love because you were already showing them love throughout their process. Treat them like the one who now loves you instead of the one who mistreated you. Don't allow your hurt to turn you into the enemy they once treated you as, but instead, love them like your brother/sister in Christ whose life was changed.

REFLECTION

This week's prayer:

Father, You are my light and salvation; whom shall I fear? You are the strength of my life; whom shall I be afraid? When the wicked come against me, let them not be successful in their pursuit. I will stand firm and will not be shaken. Give me the strength to love my enemies the way You do. Give me eyes to see them the way You do. Let me be a light in a dark place. Give me a heart of flesh towards my enemies. Bless those who curse me and help me to respond well when I am mistreated. While they are going through their process, help me to love them consistently. Let me not compromise my character but to love them despite how I am treated. Let my first response be a godly response, and let my actions be pleasing in your sight. Change the heart of those who hate me. Reveal Yourself to them and draw them close to You. Let them see the salvation of the Lord. Give them the shield of Your salvation. Encompass them with Your love. Heal their hearts. Let them see themselves the way You see them. Let them love themselves the way You love them. I trust You to take care of them. Break down their walls and let their guard down. In Jesus' name, amen.

One of the hardest yet rewarding things you can do for your enemy is pray for them. Use the space below to pray your own personal prayer for your enemy or someone you are not fond of. Pray for them as though you are praying for yourself.

_____

_____

_____

_____

_____

_____

_____

_____

_____

_____

_____

_____

_____

_____

_____

_____

_____

_____

_____

_____

_____

Come back to this space a month from now and reflect on how your prayers have changed you and them.

_____

_____

_____

_____

_____

_____

_____

_____

_____

_____

_____

_____

_____

_____

_____

_____

_____

Week 10

GOD IS SEEKING

The Lord looks down from heaven on the entire human race; he
looks to see if anyone is truly wise, if anyone seeks God.
~~Psalms 14:2 NLT~~

God is omnipresent (all present), omnipotent (all powerful), and omniscient (all knowing)! God knows, sees, and hears everything. The amazing thing is, He even knows the thoughts of the mind and the intentions of the heart. God knows whether someone's motives are pure or tainted. Nothing can be hidden from Him.

There is nothing more important to God than your relationship with Him. He sits on His throne, looks down, and examines the hearts of everyone on earth. He is looking to see if there is anyone who truly knows Him. Is there anyone who trust, fear, love, and obey Him? God is searching for those who diligently seek after Him. It's one thing to know *of* God and another to *know* Him.

The reality is some people only know God by association. For example, some people say, "I am a Christian because my mom is a Christian and I grew up in church." For them, it was a thing to do, and as they got older, they did not continue the journey and take the time to know God for themselves. There was no "seek."

The word "seek" in this context is *dāraš* in Hebrew, which means "to seek with care; to seek God in prayer and worship; to seek with a demand; to seek with application; to allow oneself to be enquired of, consulted (only of God)." [3]

Think about when your boss demands something of you or when you tell your kids to do something. The intention is to get it done now and without distraction. There is an urgency. How many of us are truly *seeking* God with care, with praise and worship, with a demand, and with application? How many of us apply what we've learned in our time of seeking? Is there an urgency in your seek? Does your soul long for God as the deer long for streams of water? Does your soul thirst for the living God (Psalms 42:1-2)?

That is the type of person God is looking for. He doesn't want to be an afterthought or to be penciled into your schedule. He wants all of you. He wants you to desire Him. He wants to be your first and your last. He wants to be your everything. He cares about every detail of your life and wants to be included in it. He is sitting on His throne looking down searching the hearts of His beloved to see who is truly wise and seeks after Him. Will you be the one He finds?

REFLECTION

Take 30 minutes or more a day to seek God in worship, sitting in silence and listening, singing, dancing, or drawing. At the end, write your experience.

Day 1:
_____
_____
_____

Day 2:
_____
_____
_____

Day 3:
_____
_____
_____

Day 4:
_____
_____
_____

Day 5:
_____
_____
_____

Day 6:
_____
_____
_____

Day 7:
_____
_____
_____

Week 11

NOT IMPORTANT ENOUGH?

The members of the council were amazed when they saw the
boldness of Peter and John, for they could see that they were
ordinary men with no special training in the Scriptures. They
also recognized them as men who had been with Jesus.
~~Acts 4:13 NLT~~

In today's society, we see the twelve disciples as these powerful men of God, but back then, some people saw them as ordinary nobodies who were full of trouble. They didn't care about titles or what miracles they could perform. They didn't think they were better than anybody because they were the chosen twelve. They just loved the Lord and they wanted to share Him with everybody at any cost. First Corinthians 1:27-28 (AMP) says, "But God has selected [for His purpose] the foolish things of the world to shame the wise [revealing their ignorance], and God has selected [for His purpose] the weak things of the world to shame the things which are strong [revealing their frailty]. God has selected [for His purpose] the insignificant (base) things of the world, and the things that are despised *and* treated with contempt, [even] the things that are nothing, so that He might reduce to nothing the things that are."

God wants you to love Him and put Him first above anything else. He wants your yes and for you to fulfill your purpose with boldness. God has put His Words in your mouth (Isaiah 51:16, Jeremiah 1:9). You have faith in Jesus Christ who promised the gift of the Holy Spirit who lives in you. "Or do you not know that your body is the temple of the Holy Spirit *who* is in you, whom you have from God, and you are not your own?" (1 Corinthians 6:19 NKJV). God is the same yesterday, today, and forever. You follow the same God as the disciples. You are filled with the same Spirit the disciples were filled with. You have the same power within you that they did.

You may see yourself as just an ordinary person, a nobody, or someone who goes unnoticed, but you have the power of God within you! You are somebody who is filled with the Holy Spirit. You have a purpose, and you are so much more powerful than you think. You are not just important enough, but you are more than enough! You have a purpose and you have what it takes to do great things for God.

REFLECTION

It's time to take back your identity. Cancel those word curses and affirm yourself. Write down ways you were bold, stepped out of your comfort zone, or worked on your goals. You are important. You are enough. You have a purpose.

Day 1:
_____
_____
_____

Day 2:
_____
_____
_____

Day 3:
_____
_____
_____

Day 4:
_____
_____
_____

Day 5:
_____
_____
_____

Day 6:
_____
_____
_____

Day 7:
_____
_____
_____

Week 12

PUTTING IN THE WORK

....Be faithful until death, and I will give you the crown of life.
~~Revelation 2:10 NKJV~~

When you are on a team, and you win a competition, game, or tournament, you are rewarded with a trophy or medal. In order to win, each member has to do their part. They can't just show up to practice once a week and expect to be put in the game, get better, operate in excellence or win; they have to put in their own personal time.

If you are an ice skater, you go to the ice rink several times a week to practice by yourself. If you are a basketball player, you go to a local park or gym. With baseball, you go to the batting cage. Dancers have to stretch and practice their choreography at home during the week. If you don't put in the work and you're the weakest one on the team, guess what? You're going to be the bench warmer. Everyone wants to be used but not everybody wants to put in the work.

Revelation 2:10 tells us to be faithful until death, and God will give us the crown of life. Crown is translated from the Greek word, *stephanos*, which means, "the eternal blessedness which will be given as a prize to the genuine servants of God and Christ: the crown (wreath) which is the reward of the righteousness." [4]

Your crown is your reward, but you cannot get it unless you have been faithful ... even until death. It takes more than just attending church once a week or only on holidays. This walk with Christ is a commitment. It takes work, discipline, and dedication. The real work is at home in your secret place where nobody else can see you. It takes 3-6 years for an oyster to produce a single pearl *good enough to be used* in jewelry. A diamond has to go through heat and pressure. Nobody sees the process, but everyone can see the end result. It's not about being seen in public but it's about your own personal process and what takes place in private.

That's what God sees ... your alone time with Him – when you fall on your face in prayer and worship, when you fast outside of a corporate schedule, when you diligently read and study the Bible on your own, when you're trying your hardest to become a doer of the Word, and when praises flow from your heart throughout the day. Attending church and serving on a ministry is great, but your intimate time with God is what matters the most. That kind of faithfulness will get you the crown of life.

REFLECTION

This week's prayer:

Lord, thank You that I have another day to spend time in Your presence. You deserve all of me without any distractions. Clear my mind so I can focus completely on You. Help me to be faithful to You, not just in this moment but every second of every day. I want to do better. As the deer pants for streams of water, so my soul pants for You oh God. I want to give You all of me. Here I am completely open and ready to pour into You as You pour into me. Let there be an exchange as we dine together. In Jesus' name, amen.

This week, get in your secret place and be diligent about putting in the work and being faithful to God. Spending time with God shouldn't feel like a chore, and it's not about getting anything in return. He just wants your heart and your time. Get into a quiet environment and use the space below to journal your intimate time or conversation with God.

_____

_____

_____

_____

_____

_____

_____

_____

_____

_____

_____

_____

_____

_____

_____

_____

_____

_____

_____

Week 13

WALKING IN YOUR ASSIGNMENT

"Look! The cry of the people of Israel has reached me, and I have seen
how harshly the Egyptians abuse them. Now go, for I am sending you
to Pharaoh. You must lead my people Israel out of Egypt." But Moses
protested to God, "Who am I to lead the people of Israel out of Egypt?"
~~Exodus 3:9-11 NLT~~

Moses thought he was inadequate to handle such a big assignment from God. He
was just an ordinary man raising his family and taking care of his father-in-law's
flock. He also fled from Egypt years prior for killing an Egyptian for beating a
fellow Israelite. Going back to Egypt to lead the Israelites out of slavery and into
a land flowing with milk and honey sounded unreasonable to Moses. How much
could he really accomplish upon his return? Who would take him seriously? How
would he be able to get a whole nation of people to listen to him?

Has God given you an assignment that you haven't pursued because you felt as
though you are not good enough? Like Moses, do you feel inadequate to handle
the task God has given you because you think someone who is spiritually more
mature could accomplish it better than you? Don't worry! In the following verse
(12), God told Moses, "I will be with you...." Still in doubt, Moses wanted to
know what he should say if the Israelites questioned him. In verse 14, "God said
to Moses, "I AM WHO I AM." And he said, "Say this to the people of Israel, 'I
AM has sent me to you."

If God has given you an assignment, He will give you the right tools (words,
strategies, action plans, or blueprints) to accomplish His will. He won't send you
out like a deer in headlights. For those of you who know this story, you are aware
of the struggle and persecution that Moses endured before he was able to lead the
people of Israel out of Egypt. Once they were out of Egypt, Moses then had to
deal with the Israelites' rebellious hearts. As a result, an eleven-day journey in
the wilderness ended up as a forty-year curse.

Just because God is calling you to do something, doesn't mean it's going to be
easy – it just means God is with you and will give you the tools and strength you
need to overcome and accomplish God's will for your life. Sometimes God will
put you in humbling situations so you won't take credit for what He has done.
People will know that it was only by the grace of God that brought you through so
He can get the glory. Have faith and walk in the assignment God has given you.

REFLECTION

This week's declaration:
I will not walk in fear. I have power, love, and a sound mind! I have everything I need to do what God has called me to do. I have the heart and boldness to accomplish all that God created me for. I will be faithful and endure to the end.

Go through the assignments God has given you that you have not completed or started. Ask yourself, "why haven't I started?" Or "why haven't I completed it?" Maybe it isn't the right time. Maybe it's fear. Could it be lack of resources?

If you haven't started because of fear, I want to encourage you to release that fear over to God. God has not given you the spirit of fear, but He has given you power, love, and a sound mind (2 Timothy 1:7). Don't let the enemy rob you of your obedience and blessings. You have nothing to fear because God is on your side. He is waiting for you to walk in faith and take the next step.

Assignment(s) God has given you:

_____

_____

_____

_____

What is preventing you from starting or completing your assignment(s):

_____

_____

_____

_____

What can you do to move forward or what steps can you take?

_____

_____

_____

_____

Week 14

TRUE WORSHIP

God *is* Spirit, and those who worship Him must worship in spirit and truth.
~~John 4:24 NKJV~~

When some people hear the word *worship*, they automatically associate it with singing – mostly slow songs that tug on their hearts. However, worship is more than that! The first time the word *worship* appears in the New Testament, it is found in Matthew 2:2 when the wise men went to Jerusalem to see Jesus, the newborn Savior. The scripture states, "Where is He who has been born King of the Jews? For we have seen His star in the east and have come to worship Him" (AMP). The word *worship* is translated from the Greek word *proskyneō* which means:

1. To kiss the hand to (towards) one, in token of reverence.
2. Among the Orientals, esp. the Persians, to fall upon the knees and touch the ground with the forehead as an expression of profound reverence.
3. In the NT by kneeling or prostration to do homage (to one) or make obeisance, whether in order to express respect or to make supplication.[5]

According to the original biblical context of worship, it has nothing to do with singing at all, but it has everything to do with how you show respect towards God. To worship God means to reverence Him. It means to fall on your knees and touch the ground with your forehead. To worship God means to kneel or lay prostrate in the presence of God.

When Satan tempted Jesus in Matthew 4:9, Satan said he would give Jesus all the kingdoms of the world and their glory if He would *fall down* and worship him. Satan wanted Jesus to kneel before him and express reverence to him in worship, but Jesus rebuked Satan and sent him away.

Yes, you can sing, express words of gratitude, pray in tongues, or weep while in those positions, but to worship God is a position one takes as a sign of respect and reverence. Worship is also a heart's posture as well. If you are not able to kneel down due to physical limitations or because of the environment you are in (e.g. work or in your car), you can reverence God, express respect or make supplication to God in your heart. Something profound happens when you truly worship God in spirit and in truth!

REFLECTION

Be intentional about worshipping God. How did you express your worship? What was your experience? Did you feel a difference during your time of worship?

Day 1:

_____

_____

_____

Day 2:

_____

_____

_____

Day 3:

_____

_____

_____

Day 4:

_____

_____

_____

Day 5:

_____

_____

_____

Day 6:

_____

_____

_____

Day 7:

_____

_____

_____

Week 15

THANKSGIVING

"Gather to me my faithful ones, who made a covenant with me by sacrifice!"
The heavens declare his righteousness, for God himself is judge! *Selah* "Hear, O
my people, and I will speak; O Israel, I will testify against you. I am God, your
God. Not for your sacrifices do I rebuke you; your burnt offerings are continually
before me. I will not accept a bull from your house or goats from your folds.
For every beast of the forest is mine, the cattle on a thousand hills. I know all
the birds of the hills, and all that moves in the field is mine. "If I were hungry, I
would not tell you, for the world and its fullness are mine. Do I eat the flesh of
bulls or drink the blood of goats? Offer to God a sacrifice of thanksgiving, and
perform your vows to the Most High, and call upon me in the day of trouble;
I will deliver you, and you shall glorify me." But to the wicked God says:
"What right have you to recite my statutes or take my covenant on your lips?
~~Psalms 50:5-16 ESV~~

In the last verse (16), God was addressing the wicked. Asaph said, "But to the
wicked God says: "...." That tells us that in verses 5-15, God was specifically
talking to His followers. God spoke against the Israelites, not because of their
sacrifices but because of *what* they were sacrificing. Biblically speaking, bulls
and goats were offered as a burnt offering, which is why God said, "I will not
accept a bull from your house or goats from your folds." Why? Because He owns
everything. If He were hungry, He could feed off anything He wants. What God
really wants is your sacrifice of thanksgiving. God does not want what is tangible,
but instead, He wants your heart – a heart of gratitude. He wants you to offer
something that is personal and irreplaceable. He wants something that will cause
you to stop what we are doing just to acknowledge Him – to bask in the splendor
of His goodness. The Bible says God inhabits the praises of His people (Psalms
22:3 NKJV), meaning He dwells in your praises. When you are feeling void or
distant from Him, you are one praise away from connecting with Him again.

Verse 14 says, "Offer to God a sacrifice of thanksgiving, and perform your vows
to the Most High." Renew your vow and covenant with God today. Give Him
a surrendered yes. Pay your vows to God with your worship. Let the sound of
praise flow from your mouth. God said, "Call upon me in the day of trouble; I will
deliver you, and you shall glorify me." The thing is, God doesn't just want you to
call on Him when you are in trouble, but He wants to be involved in every aspect
of your life. God will help you in times of trouble because He loves you, but He
wants daily intimacy. He wants a relationship with you. He cares more about you
spending quality time with Him than your sacrifice.

REFLECTION

This week, write your heart of thanksgiving, praise, and worship to the Lord.

Day 1:

_____

_____

_____

Day 2:

_____

_____

_____

Day 3:

_____

_____

_____

Day 4:

_____

_____

_____

Day 5:

_____

_____

_____

Day 6:

_____

_____

_____

Day 7:

_____

_____

_____

Week 16

PLUMB LINE

Then he showed me another vision. I saw the Lord standing beside a wall
that had been built using a plumb line. He was using a plumb line to see
if it was still straight. And the Lord said to me, "Amos, what do you see?"
I answered, "A plumb line." And the Lord replied, "I will test my people
with this plumb line. I will no longer ignore all their sins. The pagan
shrines of your ancestors will be ruined, and the temples of Israel will be
destroyed; I will bring the dynasty of King Jeroboam to a sudden end."
~~Amos 7:7-9 NLT~~

A plumb line is a tool used for determining whether or not something is perfectly
vertical and not crooked. In a spiritual sense, it was God's way of determining
the righteousness of His people when they were "crooked" or rebellious or went
astray. The Israelites are God's chosen people. He couldn't continue to sit back
and ignore their sins while they lived a lifestyle that wasn't pleasing to Him. As a
result, Amos prophesied that the people of Israel would become captives in exile
(verse 17). Even though going through God's process was difficult for Israel, it
was necessary because it was God's way of bringing them back into alignment
with Him. In Amos 9:11-15, God made a promise to restore Israel to its former
glory. He promised to bring them back to their land and give them a prosperous
and fruitful life.

Although you are under the grace of the new covenant, there may be times when
God will use a plumb line to determine if you have fallen out of alignment. God
loves you too much to leave you in your sin. Just as His name is Abba, discipline
and correction comes with being His child. He loves you too much to leave you
the same. His love chases after you.

"So Jesus told them this story: "If a man has a hundred sheep and one of them
gets lost, what will he do? Won't he leave the ninety-nine others in the wilderness
and go to search for the one that is lost until he finds it? And when he has found
it, he will joyfully carry it home on his shoulders. When he arrives, he will call
together his friends and neighbors, saying, 'Rejoice with me because I have found
my lost sheep.' In the same way, there is more joy in heaven over one lost sinner
who repents and returns to God than over ninety-nine others who are righteous
and haven't strayed away!" (Luke 15:3-7 NLT).

Nothing you do can separate you from the love of God (Romans 8:38-39). God will chase after you to get you back into alignment when you have fallen short of His glory. The process may not be easy. It will require you to repent. It may even require you to let go of some things or some people. It may hurt and you may cry or get frustrated, but God's intention is to always make sure your life points back to Him. He always wants you to be in alignment with His perfect will. Do not be discouraged or give up if you're going through a process of being tested with God's plumb line. It will come with a cost but trust the process because it is for your good!

REFLECTION

This week's prayer:

Lord, I know You want Your perfect will to be done in my life. I know there will be times when You will have to use a plumb line to align me back on the right path. It doesn't always feel good, but I will trust You through the process because I know You want the best for me. I ask that You give me wisdom and discernment to make the right choices. Let me be sensitive to Your voice, especially in times of uncertainty. Give me strength to endure when things get difficult. When I am in deep trouble, I will search for You. When I cry out to You, You will listen. Let the conviction of the Holy Spirit burn within me. Let my first response be a godly response and let everything I do be pleasing to You. By Your strong arm, You will redeem me. Your ways are holy, therefore, I will put my trust in You. In Jesus' name, amen.

This week's declaration:

I will be aligned to the perfect will of the Father for my life. I have strength to endure difficult times. I have wisdom and discernment in every situation. My ear gates are open; I can hear the voice of the Lord with clarity and certainty. My first response will be a godly response. The conviction of the Holy Spirit is within me. I will trust in the Lord with all of my heart. I will not lean on my own understanding, but in all my ways I will acknowledge the Lord so He will direct my path.

Come back and reflect on this past week. Did you have any pivotal moments where you experienced correction or realignment from God? How did it make you feel? How did you grow through it?

_____

_____

_____

_____

_____

_____

_____

_____

_____

_____

Week 17

BUT LORD, YOU DO NOT LISTEN!

How long, O Lord, must I call for help? But you do not listen! ….
~~Habakkuk 1:2 NLT~~

Before this book, we know nothing about Habakkuk. We don't know where he comes from, who his family is, how he got called to be a prophet, what brought him to this point of frustration, or how long he's been crying out to the Lord. All we know is that he is a prophet who received a vision from the Lord (Habakkuk 1:1). Here is this man of God, who can see visions, has dreams, and hear from God directly, and yet the first thing Habakkuk says is, "How long, O Lord, must I call for help? But you do not listen!" Woah! Is he frustrated or what?

Can you relate to Prophet Habakkuk? How many times have you cried out to the Lord in frustration? You've prayed. You've fasted. Yet, like Prophet Habakkuk, you convince yourself that God is not listening.

How long must I call out to You for help? How many nights do I have to cry myself to sleep? How much longer do I have to go through this before You intervene? Don't You see my tears? Don't You care about me?

When I read Habakkuk 1:2, the Lord instantly reminded me of who He is. He said, "I am Omnipotent, Omnipresent, and Omniscient!" Wow! God, You *are* all-powerful; You *do* exist everywhere at once; and You *are* all-knowing!

How can we get so caught up in our circumstances, that in a moment, we forget who He is? How quickly we forget that His grace is sufficient, and His strength is made perfect in our weaknesses! Since God is all-knowing and exist everywhere at once, how can He not hear you?

Listen to the Lord's reply to Habakkuk in chapter one verse five, "Look around at the nations; look and be amazed! For I am doing something in your own day, something you wouldn't believe even if someone told you about it."

He hears your prayers. He sees your tears. Trust that God is working on your behalf. Trust that His plans for your life are to prosper you and not harm you, but to give you hope and a future. Trust that God is going to do something in your life – something so amazing that you wouldn't believe it even if someone told you! Rest in Him and His promises over your life.

REFLECTION

This week's prayer:

God, sometimes I feel as though You are not listening, but I know in my heart that You are. You are Omnipresent and Omniscient. Forgive me for doubting the essence of who You are. I may not be able to see You working everything out for my good, but I trust that You are. I release (emotion) to You. Let there be a great exchange for Your peace and joy. Thank You for always listening and being there for me. In Jesus' name, amen.

Sometimes, our emotions get the best of us and cloud our thoughts and judgements. Breathe! Use the space below to journal and release your emotions over to God this week. Don't limit yourself to just words if you want to express yourself in a different manner such as your own song or drawing.

_____

_____

_____

_____

_____

_____

_____

_____

_____

_____

_____

_____

_____

_____

_____

_____

_____

_____

_____

_____

_____

Week 18

TIME TO REAP JOY

We laughed and laughed and overflowed with gladness. We were
left shouting for joy and singing your praise. All the nations saw it
and joined in, saying, "The Lord has done great miracles for them!"
Yes, he did mighty miracles and we are overjoyed! Now, Lord, do it
again! Restore us to our former glory! May streams of your refreshing
flow over us until our dry hearts are drenched again. Those who sow
their tears as seeds will reap a harvest with joyful shouts of glee.
They may weep as they go out carrying their seed to sow, but they
will return with joyful laughter and shouting with gladness as they
bring back armloads of blessings and a harvest overflowing!
~~Psalms 126:2-6 TPT~~

Maybe you're in a season of sorrow. It seems like everything around you is falling
apart. Maybe things on your job are turning upside down. Maybe you received bad
news from the doctor. Maybe your marriage is on the rocks. You're drowning in
your sorrow. You go to bed crying, and you wake up with barely enough strength
to get out of bed.

Like the Israelites, you remember your days of old that were filled with laughter
and gladness. You were overjoyed at the things God did in your life. You basked in
liberty and peace. Like the Israelites, your heart cries out to God to restore you to
your former glory. Oh, how you wish things would go back to the way they were.

But there is hope! God is with you and He is on your side. He not only sees your
tears but He counts them, and He wipes them away. "You keep track of all my
sorrows. You have collected all my tears in your bottle. You have recorded each
one in your book" (Psalms 56:8 NLT).

Yes, it hurts now, and you feel like the storm will never clear, but this will not last
forever. This pain is temporary. God loves you and He cares about every detail of
your being. God will drench your heart with joy again. Matter of fact, you will reap a
harvest of it! You may go out crying but you will return with joyful laughter and shouts
of gladness as you bring back *armloads* of blessings and an overflow of harvest! There
are two things the enemy can't steal from you, and that is joy and peace that only
comes from the Holy Spirit. Rest son. Rest daughter. Abba's shalom is with you, and
the comfort of Holy Spirit is in you. May God restore the joy of your salvation and may
you be filled with the hope and love of the Father once again. Better days are ahead.

REFLECTION

Throughout the book of Psalms, we see many examples of David praising God in the mist of hardship and pain. He said in Psalms 66:17 (NLT), "For I cried out to him for help, praising him as I spoke." Use the space below to pour out your heart to the Father, praising Him along the way. It may not seem like it now, but there are so many things to praise God for. He is still good despite of!

_____

_____

_____

_____

_____

_____

_____

_____

_____

_____

_____

_____

_____

_____

_____

_____

_____

_____

_____

_____

_____

_____

_____

_____

Week 19

WHINE MUCH?

Then the foreign rabble who were traveling with the Israelites began to crave the good things of Egypt. And the people of Israel also began to complain. "Oh, for some meat!" they exclaimed. "We remember the fish we used to eat for free in Egypt. And we had all the cucumbers, melons, leeks, onions, and garlic we wanted. But now our appetites are gone. All we ever see is this manna!"
~~Numbers 11:4-6 NLT~~

"And say to the people, 'Purify yourselves, for tomorrow you will have meat to eat. You were whining, and the Lord heard you when you cried, "Oh, for some meat! We were better off in Egypt!" Now the Lord will give you meat, and you will have to eat it. And it won't be for just a day or two, or for five or ten or even twenty. You will eat it for a whole month until you gag and are sick of it. For you have rejected the Lord, who is here among you, and you have whined to him, saying, "Why did we ever leave Egypt?"
~~Numbers 11:18-20 NLT~~

Sometimes we ask God for things we want or think we need just to satisfy our desires. We don't want to wait for God's timing or accept no for an answer. We can't see in the moment that God has something better for us. We lose patience and get frustrated with the process.

God's plan was to bring the Israelites to a land flowing of milk and honey – a land God promised to their ancestors. They were going in circles in the wilderness because of their rebellion and disobedience. The journey became long and discouraging. They lost sight of all that God did to bring them out of Egypt. They lost sight of the promise. They lost sight of who God is – a Covenant Keeper, a Way Maker, a Provider.

We become so desperate. Lord, please send my spouse. Lord, please bless me with another job. Lord, increase my anointing. Lord, use me ... Lord! Lord! Lord! We don't sit still in His presence long enough to hear His answer so we whine, beg, and plead with God for the same thing day after day. Then when God gives us what we begged for, we can't handle it, we get sick of it, or we end up being miserable and hating it.

God will never withhold any good thing from you (Psalms 84:11). Just because He said no or wait, doesn't mean He doesn't love you. It means you're not ready for it yet or that He has something better in store for you. He has everything under control. He knows what you need when you need it. He knows the deepest desires of your heart. He knows the things you long for the most. After all, He created you. Stop trying to help God by controlling or manipulating the situation. Do not compromise your faith or integrity to get what you want. You will end up hating the thing you so desperately wanted when you finally get it because you received it outside of God's timing. God knows what you need, and He will bless You with *His* best in *His* perfect timing. He will make everything beautiful in its own time (Ecclesiastes 3:11). Trust God and let Him do what He does best.

REFLECTION

This week's prayer:

Father, things are not going the way I planned. I acknowledge that I have tried to figure things out on my own. I ask that You forgive me for being impatient with your timing and process. I repent for not trusting Your plan for my life and trying to do things my way. Give me the strength to accept Your "no" because I know that You have something better planned for me. Your plans for my life are to prosper me and not harm me. Help me to remember that Your plans give me hope for a better future. Give me patience to go through the process of waiting. Things will not always be as they are, so I surrender to Your will and renew my "yes" to You again today. God, I will not control or try to manipulate You because I trust You. In Jesus' name, amen.

Sometimes situations can bring you to a place of desperation. Financial hardships, health problems, family issues, or not being where you want to be in life can wear you out. You try to figure it out on your own and look for solutions from other people instead of turning to God first. What are you worried about? What are you longing for in this moment? Release it over to God and renew your trust in Him.

_____

_____

_____

_____

_____

_____

_____

_____

_____

_____

_____

_____

_____

_____

_____

_____

_____

_____

Week 20

NOT FORGOTTEN

You are not forgotten, for you have been chosen and destined by Father God.
The Holy Spirit has set you apart to be God's holy ones, obedient followers
of Jesus Christ who have been gloriously sprinkled with his blood. May
God's delightful grace and peace cascade over you many times over!
~~1 Peter 1:2 TPT~~

God is very precise and detailed. Don't believe me? Read Exodus and Leviticus.
God gave very specific details instructions regarding the construction of the Ark
of the Covenant, including its design, what the priests should wear, what, how
and when to sacrifice an offering, and how to purify oneself to come into His
presence. You think God has forgotten about you? Think again! He was very
careful in creating and molding you into the perfect image of Himself. He even
knows every strand of hair on your head (Matthew 10:30-31 NLT).

When you think nobody else cares, God certainly does. You, yes you! You are on
the mind and heart of God every second of every day. David said, "Every single
moment you are thinking of me! How precious and wonderful to consider that you
cherish me constantly in your every thought! O God, your desires towards me are
more than the grains of sand on every shore! When I awake each morning, you're
still with me" (Psalms 139:17-18 TPT).

God calls you His own. You are His precious son/daughter. You are the apple of
His eye. His love for you runs deeper than any human can ever love you. Although
God is not far from you, His desire is for you to seek Him, to reach out to Him,
and to find Him. For in Him, you live and move and have your being because you
are His offspring (Acts 17:27-28).

Nothing you do can ever separate you from the love of God. He loves you despite
your flaws, mistakes, rebellion, and sin. In all of His perfection, He knew every
decision you were going to make. Even if you mess up, fall short of His glory,
or sin, His hand is never too far from your reach and His ear is never closed off
from you. All you have to do is repent. Repentance will draw you back into close
intimacy with the Father and bring you back into alignment with His will. God's
promises for your life are still yes and amen. God's timing is perfect and His plans
for your life are prosperous, secure, and full of hope. "For I know the plans I have
for you," declares the Lord, "plans to prosper you and not harm you, plans to give
you hope and a future" (Jeremiah 29:11 NIV).

Rest in the love of the Father and be secure in your identity as a son or daughter. You are *not* forgotten. You *have* been chosen and destined by God. The Holy Spirit *has* set you apart to be God's holy one. You *have* been created to be an obedient follower of Jesus who gloriously sprinkled you with His blood. May God's delightful grace and peace cascade over you many times over!

REFLECTION

This week's prayer:

Lord, thank You for creating me in Your image. Forgive me for thinking of myself as less than. Being called Your son/daughter is a privilege and an honor, and sometimes I take it for granted. Please forgive me. You care about every detail of my life. When I feel lonely and forgotten, it is a lie from the enemy. You have never left me. You have always been there with me and You always will. I thank You because You have great plans for me even if I don't see it now. I trust the work You are doing in my life. You have never failed me and You never will. I trust You with my whole heart. I love You, Lord. Amen.

This week's declaration:

I am not forgotten. I was made in the image and likeness of God, and I am my Father's child. I am the child of the Most High God. I am loved. I am special. I am important to the body of Christ and I am needed. God is not done with me yet. I am gifted. I am talented. I am sanctified and anointed. I have a purpose and God's plans for my life are great.

Proverbs 18:21 (NKJV) says, "Death and life are in the power of the tongue, and those who love it will eat its fruit." There is no better way to combat the lies of the enemy than to affirm yourself with the Word of God. This week, find scriptures that you can speak over yourself that will affirm you and break off every word curse that you or someone else spoke over you. Speak those scriptures every day and mediate on them throughout the day.

_____

_____

_____

_____

_____

_____

_____

_____

_____

_____

_____

_____

_____

_____

Week 21

OBEYING GOD

This is the message the Lord gave Jeremiah when Jehoiakim son of
Josiah was king of Judah: "Go to the settlement where the families
of the Recabites live, and invite them to the Lord's Temple. Take
them into one of the inner rooms, and offer them some wine."
~~Jeremiah 35:1-2 NLT~~

Then the Lord gave this message to Jeremiah: "This is what the Lord of
Heaven's Armies, the God of Israel, says: Go and say to the people in Judah
and Jerusalem, 'Come and learn a lesson about how to obey me. The Recabites
do not drink wine to this day because their ancestor Jehonadab told them not
to. But I have spoken to you again and again, and you refuse to obey me.
~~Jeremiah 35:12-14 NLT~~

In Jeremiah 35, the Lord told Jeremiah to go to the house of the Recabites, bring them
to the Temple, and offer them wine to drink. However, they refused to drink because
their ancestors commanded them not to. The Lord then told Jeremiah to go back to
the Recabites and warn them of the disaster that would come upon them because of
their disobedience. Throughout the book of Jeremiah, God persistently sent prophets
to Judah and Jerusalem to tell them to turn away from their sin, stop serving other
gods, repent, and obey God, but they did not listen. Because they obeyed their earthly
father and not their heavenly Father, disaster was going to fall on them.

Here is the lesson: we obey the laws of man, we drop what we are doing for our
bosses, and we obey our parents. However, when God tells us to do something,
we hesitate or convince ourselves that it was the enemy because God couldn't
have possibly told us to do such a thing. Other times, we are bold in our response
and tell God no just like the Recabites. Disobeying God has consequences. God
created us. We are living to fulfill His will and purpose for our lives, not vice
versa. How dare we tell God no or allow fear to grip us to a point of dormancy.

Sometimes, God wants you to take risks. Sometimes, He wants to test your faith
to help you grow and to launch you into something greater. Without faith it is
impossible to please God (Hebrews 11:6). Having faith is hard at times, especially
when your flesh looks at your current situation and makes you uncomfortable.
Sometimes, it's hard when you're faced with the impossible, but that is what faith
is. You put limitations on God when He wants nothing more than to bless you far
more than what you can imagine.

If you feel as though God is telling you to do something but you are still looking for confirmation, continue to pray about it, but not to the extent of using it as an excuse out of fear. However, if you are absolutely sure that God is telling to do something, trust Him and take that leap of faith. Do not be like the Recabites in your refusal to obey God. Even when people and life circumstances tells you not to, do it anyway because there are blessings on the other side of your obedience. Remember, delayed obedience is still disobedience.

REFLECTION

This week's prayer:

God, I thank You for allowing me to see another day. I do not take it for granted because I know some people didn't make it. That means You are not done with me and I still have a purpose to fulfill. I submit my day to You. I pray You teach me how to be a good steward of my time. I don't want to leave this earth without fulfilling my purpose. I pray that You reveal to me Your plans for my life. Give me strategies and blueprints and the wisdom to carry it out. Let me not get so caught up in obeying man, that I miss being obedient to You. Connect me with the right people and give me doors of opportunities. I want to live a life pleasing to You and not man. I want You to be my first priority. Wherever You want me to go, I will go. Whatever You want me to say, I will say. Whatever You want me to do, I will do. Give me the strength to step out on faith. I give You my yes because I trust You. Father, let Your will be done on earth in my life as it is in heaven. In Jesus' name, amen.

You cannot obey God's voice if you do not recognize it. God speaks to everyone differently. Some people have dreams and visions, some hear Him audibly, others hear God in their spirit, but everyone hears God through the Word.

Have you ever had a gut feeling that something was wrong? Have you ever said, "Something told me not to do this, and I'm so glad I listened."? Guess what? That nudge, gut feeling, or instinct is the Holy Spirit. That is the still small voice of God. His voice is so prevalent to your every day life and purpose. This week, be intentional about listening for the voice of God and document it. How did He speak to you? What was your response? If He told you to do something, were you obedient? If so, what was the outcome? If not, why?

1.

_____

_____

_____

_____

_____

_____

_____

_____

2.

_____

_____

_____

_____

_____

_____

_____

3.

_____

_____

_____

_____

_____

_____

_____

4.

_____

_____

_____

_____

_____

_____

_____

Week 22

PROTECT THE SEED

But that night as the workers slept, his enemy came and planted weeds
among the wheat, then slipped away. When the crop began to grow and
produce grain, the weeds also grew. The farmer's workers went to him and
said, 'Sir, the field where you planted that good seed is full of weeds! Where
did they come from?' "'An enemy has done this!' the farmer exclaimed.
~~Matthew 13:25-28 NLT~~

Have you ever had a dream or an idea, but you dismissed it because you
thought it was impossible or the vision was too big, or maybe you thought
you weren't good enough? God has planted seeds in each of us. Sometimes
we think the idea is too big or impossible. Sometimes, we don't even think
we are worthy enough to fulfill such a big assignment. Surely, God made a
mistake. Matter of fact, it wasn't from God at all; it was a lie from hell. Admit
it... there have been times when you rebuked the will of God and blamed it
on the enemy. But behold, God does not make mistakes! There is absolutely
nothing too big for Him. It may be too big for *you*, but if you can do it in your
own strength, it's not big enough for God. Being in the will of God, even if it
seems impossible, means you do not have to figure it out on your own or do
it in your own strength. Do not worry or be dismayed. God will give you the
blueprint, along with strategies, resources, and connections you will need to
fulfill His will and purpose for your life.

When God plants a seed in your heart, it is up to you to take care of it and protect
it so it will not be contaminated, crushed, destroyed, or end up dead. Just as God
can plant good seeds, the enemy can also plant seeds of doubt, fear, frustration,
and discouragement. The enemy wants nothing more than to destroy the seed that
God planted in you before it even beings to manifest. What dreams, visions, or
ideas did God give you? Did you ignore it? Did you rebuke it and blame it on the
enemy? If so, repent and ask God to restore the seed. If God placed something
in you, that means He trust *you* to fulfill the assignment. What an honor and a
privilege to be considered and used by God!

Here is what you can do to protect and care for your seed and see it to completion:

1. Write the vision (Habakkuk 2:2-3 NET).
2. Fast (Matthew 6:17-18 AMP).
3. Pray continually (1 Thessalonians 5:17 NKJV).
4. Don't allow people to have a negative impact over you. Sometimes the best thing to do is be silent until the work is done (Proverbs 21:23 TPT; 1 Thessalonians 4:11-12 TPT).
5. Only tell people you trust so they can pray with you and keep you accountable (1 Corinthians 4:2 TPT; Matthew 18:19-20 NKJV; Proverbs 27:17 NKJV).
6. Cast down every imagination of doubt, fear, and insecurity (2 Corinthians 10:5 KJV, TPT).
7. Resist the devil and he will flee (James 4:7 NKJV).

REFLECTION

Has God planted something in your life? Did someone encourage you to pursue a thing because they noticed something in you? Is there something that comes naturally easy to you that you thought nobody else would care about? Has more than one person told you that you are good at something and suggested you do something with it? Have you had reoccurring dreams or ideas that you cannot seem to shake? Maybe you're good at writing or drawing. Maybe you are really good at organizing. Maybe you like decorating. Maybe you're good at teaching, sewing, baking, taking pictures, dancing, video editing, or encouraging others. The list can go on. Those little details are seeds that God has planted in you.

This week, think about the seeds God has planted in you. Once you realize what they are, begin protecting them by interceding and asking God what to do with it and begin to plow.

Ask yourself these questions: What seed(s) did God plant in me? What did I do with them? How did I respond? What steps can I take to begin to fulfill my God-given purpose?

Week 23

WAITING ON GOD

The Lord said to Moses, "Come up to me on the mountain and wait there, that I may give you the tablets of stone, with the law and the commandments, which I have written for their instruction."
~~Exodus 24:12 ESV~~

The glory of the Lord dwelt on Mount Sinai, and the cloud covered it six days. And on the seventh day he called to Moses out of the midst of the cloud.
~~Exodus 24:16 ESV~~

In this passage, God told Moses to meet and wait for Him on Mount Sinai so He could give him tablets of stone with the commandments on them. Moses did not have a television, a tablet, videos games, or a cell phone to keep him occupied. Moses waited for God on the mountain for seven days before God actually spoke to him. Moses didn't get weary in waiting because he had intimacy and fellowship with the Lord. Moses was content in waiting.

Moses knew why he was waiting on the mountain, but he didn't know for how long. How many of you would have started to question whether you heard God's voice correctly? How many of you would've lost patience and given up? Waiting on God is not always easy. It takes patience and trust. There are examples in the Bible when God responded immediately, but there were other times when God had people waiting months or even years before responding. How many times have someone said to you, "we need to talk."? You start to get anxious wondering what the person wants to talk about. The suspense starts to get to you because you don't like to wait. Often times, you start making up scenarios about what the person wants to talk about. You get impatient and want to have the conversation right there in that moment, but you can't … you have to wait.

The question is will you wait on God in obedience, or allow the enemy to get in your head? Will you wait on God, or will you allow impatience to get the best of you and cause you to make an impulsive decision? What does God have you waiting on? Do you want to remain in the will of God, or will you choose to operate in rebellion, leading to a road of nothingness in an attempt to do something in your own strength? Don't be too hasty to give up. The moment you decide to give up could actual be the very day you receive a breakthrough or an answer. Psalms 27:14 (AMP) says, "Wait for and confidently expect the Lord; Be strong and let your heart take courage; yes, wait for and confidently expect the Lord." The best place to be while waiting is in fellowship with the Father.

REFLECTION

This week's prayer:

God, I worship You just for who You are. You are holy, majestic, and glorious. You are all powerful, ever-present, and all-knowing. No one can compare to You. Father, You exist outside of time, and although I may not always understand or see the end result, I will trust You. Give me patience to endure the waiting process. You know what's best for me. Your Word says, those that wait on the Lord shall renew their strength, therefore, I will wait on Your timing. When my mind starts to wander and I start to doubt, realign my focus back to You. In Jesus' name, amen.

This week's declarations:

I am patient. I have the peace and joy of Christ. My discernment is sharp and I can hear from God. I walk by faith and not by sight. I am satisfied with my life. I live a surrendered life. I am fearless and courageous. I am obedient to God's Word. My life is full and complete in Christ Jesus. I am not double-minded. I will wait on God's timing, therefore, my strength is renewed. I am focused and aligned with the will and purpose of God.

Throughout the week, write down some of your victories as you waited on the Lord.

_____

_____

_____

_____

_____

_____

_____

_____

_____

_____

_____

_____

_____

_____

_____

_____

_____

Week 24

IT IS YOURS

Then Adonijah the son of Haggith exalted himself, saying, "I will be king;" and
he prepared for himself chariots and horsemen, and fifty men to run before him.
~~1 Kings 1:5 NKJV~~

And the king took an oath and said, "As the Lord lives, who has redeemed
my life from every distress, just as I swore to you by the Lord God of
Israel, saying, 'Assuredly Solomon your son shall be king after me, and
he shall sit on my throne in my place,' so I certainly will do this day.
~~1 Kings 1:29-30 NKJV~~

As a result of King David's old age, his son, Adonijah, boasted about being the next
king. He went as far as getting two men, Joab and Abiathar, to help him accomplish
his goal. Adonijah even sacrificed livestock and hosted a feast celebration in honor of
his new status. When Nathan, the prophet, and David's wife, Bathsheba, heard of this,
they brought it to his attention. Because King David promised his other son, Solomon,
that title, he immediately instructed his officials to anoint Solomon as king. Everybody
in town (who wasn't at the feast celebration) played instruments and rejoiced so loud
that the earth shook. When Adonijah was informed that Solomon was made king, he
trembled with fear and begged his brother, King Solomon, not to kill him.

There may be people in your life who are plotting to take what has been promised
to you. They may even try to turn your family and friends against you. Do not
be discouraged. What God has for you will be yours, and no one can take it from
you. Even if their attempt to steal what belongs to you becomes successful, the
Lord will redeem you. Because God gave you the blueprint, their imitation will
not prosper because it wasn't their original idea. Build anyway. What you may
consider a loss is actually a blessing in disguise.

You may not understand why God's promises for you have not manifested yet or
why things may seem to be turning against you. However, there is hope. Romans
8:28 (NLT) tells us that "God causes everything to work together for the good of
those who love God and are called according to His purpose for them." You are
favored in the eyes of the Father. His promises for your life are yes and amen. You
will rise above your circumstances and you *will* have what God promised you.
Your enemies will be made a footstool under your feet, and they will watch as God
gives you what they tried to steal from you. Jesus makes intercession for you and
the great Defender is with you. Have peace and rejoice in the face of your enemies.

REFLECTION

This week's prayer:

God, Your Word says, there is nothing covered that will not be revealed and nothing hidden that will not be known. I pray that every dark thing in my life will be exposed and come to light. Show me those who are against me. Show me those who have ill intentions. Show me those who are waiting for my downfall. Reveal those people in my life who are wolves in sheep clothing. Give me discernment and let wisdom be my portion. I know what You have for me will be mine, and no one can manipulate it or steal it from me. I pray that my integrity will speak for me when my enemies try to speak against me. Let Your light shine through me so I can be a reflection of You. Give me the strength to love those who do not love me. I pray that I will always walk in the peace and joy of God despite my circumstances because those are things the enemy cannot steal from me. I pray that I will come out victorious so that You will get the glory from my life. In Jesus' name, amen.

This week's declaration:

I do not walk in fear. I have more for me than against me. I am loved and I am important. I have the strength and courage to fulfill my purpose. Nothing or no one on earth and below can stop the plan of God for my life. I will trample over my enemies and they will be made a footstool under my feet. I am a conqueror, and I will come out victorious. What is for me will be for me. I am the daughter of the King and I am favored by God, therefore, I live a prosperous and victorious life.

Week 25

BE CONTENT WHERE GOD HAS YOU

Obviously, I'm not trying to win the approval of people, but of God.
If pleasing people were my goal, I would not be Christ's servant.
~~Galatians 1:10 NLT~~

How many times have you compared your life to someone else's? How many times did you feel like you had to dress, act, or talk a certain way to fit in? How many times did you feel as though you had to have the most recent expensive accessory or gadget or go on a fancy vacation to please someone? Social media can influence how we view other people's lives and how we see our own. We are blinded by flawed people hiding behind their mask of perfection through picture-perfect lenses. Comparison and people pleasing kills. We lose ourselves and who God called us to be trying to be someone we're not. Do not try to live up to someone else's expectations or force unrealistic expectations on yourself trying to please other people. Trying to fulfill someone's expectations of where they want you to be will wear you out because you're not living the life God wants you to live. The only person you need to please is God – that's it. Apostle Paul said it best in Galatians 1:10. He was not trying to win the approval of people. If pleasing people is more important to you than pleasing God, you have built an alter and made man your idol. Who are you living for?

It is challenging to live up to man's expectations because as humans, we fail, make mistakes, and disappoint people. Some people set too high of a standard for you that God didn't even put on you, Himself. God has you right where *He* wants you to be. Be content with where God has you. Your now is not your end. Don't let what people say or do get the best of you. Someone once told me, "Don't give a situation a platform. Take what people say or do lightly and give them an excuse because it's not that serious." And you know what? That person was right. Some people will be for you, some will be against you, and some won't see your full potential. It's okay. Why? Because God does. He accepts you for who you are. Be the best person God created you to be in this moment in time. Be your full authentic self and love yourself doing it. Learn from every mistake and take opportunities as growth. The progress may be slow, but it's necessary. Accept where you are and be content in your now.

REFLECTION

This week's prayer:
Lord, help me to be content in this season. Give me the strength to ignore the voices of those around me who want me to live up to their expectation. Help me not to be a people pleaser, but one that seeks to please Your heart. Give me strength not to doubt or be discouraged in this season. You have me right where You want me to be. Thank You because where I am is necessary in order for me to get to my next level. Give me the wisdom to learn from every mistake and grow from every opportunity. In Jesus' name, amen.

Reflect on the following questions and use the space below to write your responses. "What areas in my life am I struggling to be content with? Why am I not content with where I am or who I am? Who have I allowed to place unrealistic expectations on me? Who am I trying to please and why? What are some things I can do that will center my focus back on God and please Him?

Week 26

YOUR PAST DOES NOT DEFINE YOU

For I am the least of all the apostles. In fact, I'm not even worthy to be
called an apostle after the way I persecuted God's church. But whatever I
am now, it is all because God poured out his special favor on me— and not
without results. For I have worked harder than any of the other apostles;
yet it was not I but God who was working through me by his grace.
~~1 Corinthians 15:9-10 NLT~~

These were the words of Apostle Paul. Before becoming saved himself, he was a
former Pharisee who persecuted believers. Apostle Paul was later hated, beaten,
and arrested for his faith by the same people he once identified with and stood by.
However, because he had so much blood on his hands, he did not feel deserving of
his calling. Despite his past, God changed his life and found him worthy.

Like Apostle Paul, you may not feel worthy of your calling because of your past
mistakes. Maybe you feel persecuted by those who knew you before you were
saved. Those same people mock you, judge you, gossip and lie about you, throw
your past in your face, or try to ruin your reputation. *However*, none of that matters
because God found you in your mess, saved you, called you His own, and made
you worthy. Like Apostle Paul, God poured His special favor on you, and not
without results! It was His grace that changed your life and gave you a purpose.

You know who God called you to be and what He called you to do. Some people
may not like it or agree with it, and that's okay because it wasn't their plan to
understand. Remember, Jesus was dishonored in his hometown so He was only
able to perform a few miracles (Matthew 13:53-58). Shake the dust off your feet
and keep moving because some people from your past are not called to walk with
you in your future. God called you. You are going to make mistakes but that does
not disqualify you of your purpose. Your imperfections do not mean God cannot
use you. As an imperfect being, you need a perfect God to help you through life.

Whatever happened in the past, leave it there and focus on the now. Surround
yourself with people who will encourage you and keep you accountable. Surround
yourself with people you can be transparent and vulnerable with, even things
that may seem shameful. Surround yourself with people who will speak life into
you. There may be times in your life that if it's not people bringing you down, it's
going to be you that brings you down. When times get tough and the persecution
gets real, you may question your calling or want to give up. You cannot do life on
your own. The journey is worth it and so are you!

REFLECTION

Like Apostle Paul said, I am who I am because of God's grace and because He poured special favor on me. Apostle Paul was a product of God's grace that was evident everywhere he went. So that is my prayer for you: that God will pour out His special favor on you and that you will be a product of God's grace wherever you go.

This week's prayer:
Father, thank You for redeeming me and calling me Your own. Thank You for creating me in Your image and likeness. I am who I am because of Your grace. I am nothing without You. Your unfailing love saw beyond my imperfections and gave me a purpose. Father, You poured out Your special favor on me so I can advance the Kingdom. Give me strength to endure and persevere through trials, tribulations, and persecution. Life is not always easy and I cannot do this without You. I give You permission to reign supreme over my life as my Lord and King. I say yes to Your will, and I surrender to Your plan for my life. Let Your will be done on earth in my life as it is in heaven. In Jesus' name, amen.

This week's declarations:
My past does not define me. I can do all things through Christ who strengthens me. I am who I am because God poured out His special favor on me – and not without results! I will be unapologetically me because I am made in the image and likeness of my Father. I will be all that God created me to be. God works through me by His grace. I will press towards the mark no matter how hard things may get. I will stay focused on my God-given purpose. I am a product of God's grace wherever I go.

Week 27

POSTURE OF PRAYER

Then Elijah said to Ahab, "Go get something to eat and drink, for I hear a mighty rainstorm coming!" So Ahab went to eat and drink. But Elijah climbed to the top of Mount Carmel and bowed low to the ground and prayed with his face between his knees. Then he said to his servant, "Go and look out toward the sea." The servant went and looked, then returned to Elijah and said, "I didn't see anything." Seven times Elijah told him to go and look. Finally the seventh time, his servant told him, "I saw a little cloud about the size of a man's hand rising from the sea." Then Elijah shouted, "Hurry to Ahab and tell him, 'Climb into your chariot and go back home. If you don't hurry, the rain will stop you!'" And soon the sky was black with clouds. A heavy wind brought a terrific rainstorm, and Ahab left quickly for Jezreel.
~~1 Kings 18:41-45 NLT~~

Elijah heard the sound of an abundance of rain *before* there was even a sign of rain. He bowed down and put his face between his knees while sending his servant to look toward the sea. When the servant returned, he said "there is nothing." Elijah continued to pray on his knees and sent his servant back again. The servant returns a second time and says the same thing, "there is nothing." Again, Elijah, still on his knees praying, sends his servant a third time. The servant comes back and says, "there is nothing." Despite the lack of evidence, Elijah didn't give up. He sent his servant back seven times... still on his knees... still praying... still believing... still trusting God! Elijah *knew* he heard the sound of a mighty rainstorm coming, and he was going to stay on his knees warring until it rained. *Finally*! After the seventh time, the servant saw a cloud, and there was a great rain!

How many of you are quick to rush through prayer because you have other priorities? How many of you will pray one time, wait on God, and then give up or get upset when God doesn't answer your prayer? How many of you will stay postured in prayer until you see the hand of God move? How many of you will say, "God, I will not move until You _____."? The Bible tells us to pray without ceasing (1 Thessalonians 5:17).

Just as Elijah heard the sound of a mighty rainstorm before it started raining, you have to have faith that whatever you heard, whatever God showed you, and whatever He spoke to you will come to past. You cannot just pray one time and give up. Pray until you see the move of God. Do not allow the enemy to get in your head. God is not a man that He should lie, and He will back you up because His word does not return to Him void.

REFLECTION

Be intentional with your time with God this week. Challenge yourself to increase your time with God. Diligently press into His presence. What did God say? Did He answer any of your prayers? Did you see the move of God?

Day 1:
_____
_____
_____

Day 2:
_____
_____
_____

Day 3:
_____
_____
_____

Day 4:
_____
_____
_____

Day 5:
_____
_____
_____

Day 6:
_____
_____
_____

Day 7:
_____
_____
_____

Week 28

AN IMMEDIATE YES

As Jesus was walking beside the Sea of Galilee, he saw two brothers, Simon called Peter and his brother Andrew. They were casting a net into the lake, for they were fishermen. "Come, follow me," Jesus said, "and I will send you out to fish for people." At once they left their nets and followed him. Going on from there, he saw two other brothers, James son of Zebedee and his brother John. They were in a boat with their father Zebedee, preparing their nets. Jesus called them, and immediately they left the boat and their father and followed him.
~~Matthew 4:18-22 NIV~~

When Jesus saw Peter and Andrew, He told them to follow Him. The brothers then left their nets *at once*. James and John left their boat *and* their father *immediately*. When Jesus first called these men, they did not question His identity or His intentions. They did not hesitate to drop everything they knew and loved to follow Him.

How many of you hesitate when God tells you to do something? You start to question whether it was really from God. Sometimes, you'll even go as far as blaming the enemy. "Oh, that's not from God! The devil is a liar!" Think about Ruth and Orpah in the book of Ruth. They both loved Naomi and wept aloud when she urged them to go back to their homeland. But after thinking about it, Orpah realized the sacrifice was too much so she left Naomi and went back home. Ruth, on the other hand, dropped everything she knew to follow Naomi. She left her comfort zone, family, and friends to be with Naomi in a foreign land with new people, new customs, new traditions, and a new culture. She was a widow so she didn't have a husband to support her financially. A lot was at risk, and she could have easily counted the cost, blamed the enemy, and went back home, but she didn't! She trusted the God that Naomi served and left everything *at once* and *followed* Naomi *immediately*.

Too many times we count the cost or won't sacrifice the thing God told us to lay at the altar. We won't relinquish our fears, doubts, insecurities, pride, and unforgiveness to God, preventing us from trusting Him wholeheartedly and doing what He tells us to do. Remember, delayed obedience is still disobedience. When Jesus calls you, answer. When God gives you an assignment, do it. Don't count the cost. Don't worry about your finances. Don't worry about the details. Just trust God! All He is looking for is a willing and obedient heart, and He will take care of the rest.

REFLECTION

This week's prayer:
Lord, I'm sorry for all of the times I counted the cost instead of trusting You. You have great plans for me, and I want to fulfill everything You have for me. Forgive me for choosing my own path. You are the Redeemer of time, so be gracious to me and put me back on the road that leads to You and the purpose You have for me. I want to fulfill the calling You have given me. I will no longer count the cost. Where You tell me to go, I will go. What You tell me to do, I will do. What You want me to say, I will say. Arms open wide, I surrender. Arms lifted high, I'm diving in. I give You my yes. In Jesus' name, amen.

This week's declaration:
I will do what God has called me to do. I will walk in my purpose and destiny today. Doors will be opened on my behalf. The keys of the Kingdom are in my hand. I have everything I need to do what God has called me to do. Today, I close my ears to the lies of the enemy, and I shut the mouth of Satan. I will not be afraid, and I will walk in obedience and boldness. I will not hesitate. I will give God my yes.

What did God tell you to do that has caused you to hesitate or delay? What is preventing you from giving God an immediate yes? What is causing you not to trust God wholeheartedly? Release it to God, leave it at the altar, and be obedient. Did you do it? Sometimes it's a process. What steps can you take, if necessary, to complete what God told you to do?

_____

_____

_____

_____

_____

_____

_____

_____

_____

_____

_____

_____

_____

Week 29

PROVISION

Then the Lord said to Elijah, "Go to the east and hide by Kerith Brook, near where it enters the Jordan River. Drink from the brook and eat what the ravens bring you, for I have commanded them to bring you food." So Elijah did as the Lord told him and camped beside Kerith Brook, east of the Jordan. The ravens brought him bread and meat each morning and evening, and he drank from the brook.
~~1 Kings 17:2-6 NLT~~

Nothing is impossible for God. Provision, itself, is just something He does just like a natural parent. He knows your needs before you even ask Him, and you don't have to beg. God provides for you because you are His child.

God commanded Elijah to drink from the brook and eat what the ravens brought him. First Kings 17 continues to tell us that the brook eventually dried up and God told Elijah to go to Zarephath where He commanded a widow to feed him. However, once he arrived, Elijah discovered that the widow was down to her last. She had enough for one last meal for her and her son. She made up in her mind that they were going to die of starvation. Why in the world would God send Elijah to a lady who was barely making it, herself, to feed him?

Elijah told the widow, "Don't be afraid! Go ahead and do just what you've said, but make a little bread for me first. Then use what's left to prepare a meal for yourself and your son. For this is what the Lord, the God of Israel, says: There will always be flour and olive oil left in your containers until the time when the Lord sends rain and the crops grow again!" (1 Kings 17:13-14 NLT).

At the end of it all, God blessed the widow as well! She never lacked another day of her life. God changed her circumstances in an instant! Isn't that amazing? Because she didn't look at her circumstances and was obedient, God blessed her far more than she could ask or think! That's the kind of Father you have!

You ask God to take care of this, help you with that, and provide you with this. If provision doesn't come in the form you expect it, you may risk robbing yourself of a blessing. God *tried* to provide, but you turned it away, ignored it, or didn't go where He told you to go. You cannot fathom all of who God is and you may not understand His plan. God had *birds* bring Elijah food! What may seem like a crazy plan to you, is not crazy to God at all! It's just different, and it may just as well come in a form of a raven! Next time you ask God for provision, also ask Him to help you recognize when He sends it, even if it doesn't make sense.

REFLECTION

Be attentive this week to the move of God. Document unexpected provisions, answered prayers, favor, and blessing from the Lord, and praise God for it! There is always something to be thankful for!

Day 1:
_____
_____
_____

Day 2:
_____
_____
_____

Day 3:
_____
_____
_____

Day 4:
_____
_____
_____

Day 5:
_____
_____
_____

Day 6:
_____
_____
_____

Day 7:
_____
_____
_____

Week 30

PERSECUTION IN YOUR ANOINTING

> Then the high priest and all his associates, who were members of the
> party of the Sadducees, were filled with jealousy. They arrested the
> apostles and put them in the public jail. But during the night an angel of
> the Lord opened the doors of the jail and brought them out. "Go, stand in
> the temple courts," he said, "and tell the people all about this new life."
> ~~Acts 5:17-20 NIV~~

The Sadducees were a group of wealthy religious leaders who believed the Law of Moses and had political power. Although they knew the Law, they did not have a relationship with the One who created the Law. They also did not believe in the supernatural (resurrection, heaven, hell, angels, or demons). So, when they heard the apostles boldly sharing the Gospel and saw them performing miracles and healing people, they became jealous. With all the power the Sadducees had, the power of the Holy Spirit was something they did not have. This made them battle internally with their own beliefs. Imagine their struggle: "How could any of this be possible? Jesus died on the cross. We saw it with our own eyes, but yet, His followers are still preaching, performing miracles, and healing people. I thought we ended this. All of this should have died with Jesus." It meant they would have to swallow their pride and admit that although Jesus died on the cross, His power did not. The Sadducees were so jealous of the apostles that they wanted to destroy them.

There are going to be people in your life who are going to be jealous of your anointing, gifts, calling, skills, and talents. They are so stuck in their religious mindset that they have not received the freedom to do what God has called them to do. They have not allowed the Holy Spirit to penetrate their hearts and stir up the gifts inside of them. They have not allowed God to conceive what He wants to birth in their lives. Their religious bondage has put chains on their gifts. Like the Sadducees, people may know the Bible and go to church, but they do not have the ability do what they were created to do because they have not experienced true fellowship with the Father.

They see you walking in purpose, prophesying, healing people, performing miracles, leading Bible study, hosting your own events, writing books, starting your own business, or witnessing to people. They burn with jealousy because they don't have what you have. They try to manipulate you, gossip about you, stab you in the back, and falsely accuse you so you can be rejected and cast out. They try to imitate you but fail because of their motive.

Look at what happened with Simon the sorcerer in Acts 8:18-23 (TPT). "When Simon saw how the Holy Spirit was released through the laying on of the apostles' hands, he approached them and offered them money, saying, "I want this power too. I'm willing to pay you for the anointing that you have, so that I also can lay my hands on everyone to receive the Holy Spirit." Peter rebuked him and said, "Your money will go with you to destruction! How could you even think that you could purchase God's supernatural gift with money? You will never have this gift or take part in this ministry, for your heart is not right with God. Repent this moment for allowing such wickedness to fill you. Plead with the Lord that perhaps he would forgive you the treachery of your heart. For I discern that jealous envy has poisoned you and binds you as a captive to sin."

You have something they don't have, and that is a relationship with God. They don't see your time spent in the secret place. They don't see your intimacy with the Father. You are a son/daughter. You are set apart. Acts 5:18 says they arrested the apostles and put them in jail. The Sadducees tried to stop them; they tried to bind them; they tried to destroy them, but they failed. Your anointing follows you wherever you go! Verse 19 says, "An angel of the Lord opened the doors of the jail and brought them out." Like the apostles, God will rescue you and deliver you from the hands of the enemy. You cannot be stopped!

REFLECTION

This week's prayer:
Father, despite the persecution that I may face, give me strength to continue in my calling. Help to stand firm in my faith knowing that You will rescue me from the hands of my enemies. Keep me humble in my anointing. Help me to remember that You created them and that they are still made in Your image despite how they treat me. I ask that You open the eyes of my enemies to see the truth and soften their hearts. I ask that You bless them because they do not know what they do. Free them from jealousy and religiousness. Penetrate their hearts and allow them to experience Your love in a personal way so they, too, can walk in their purpose. Thank You for everything You have done in my life. Thank You for freeing me. Thank You for anointing me and blessing me with gifts so that I can do the work You have called me to do. I am nothing without You and I live to please You. In Jesus' name, amen.

This week's declaration:
I will stand firm in my faith. I will press on despite what comes my way. I will purposely show love towards my enemies. I am the light of the world and a city on a hill that cannot be hidden. I will shine in a dark place.

In what ways have you shown love to your enemies this week?

_____

_____

_____

_____

_____

_____

_____

_____

_____

_____

_____

_____

_____

_____

_____

_____

In what ways have you been a light in a dark place or continued to walk in your purpose despite persecution?

_____

_____

_____

_____

_____

_____

_____

_____

_____

_____

_____

_____

_____

Week 31

MAKE YOUR REQUEST KNOWN

At Gibeon the Lord appeared to Solomon during the night in a dream, and God said, "Ask for whatever you want me to give you." Solomon answered, "You have shown great kindness to your servant, my father David, because he was faithful to you and righteous and upright in heart. You have continued this great kindness to him and have given him a son to sit on his throne this very day. "Now, Lord my God, you have made your servant king in place of my father David. But I am only a little child and do not know how to carry out my duties. Your servant is here among the people you have chosen, a great people, too numerous to count or number. So give your servant a discerning heart to govern your people and to distinguish between right and wrong. For who is able to govern this great people of yours?"
~~1 Kings 3:5-9 NIV~~

In 1 Kings 3, the Lord told King Solomon to ask for whatever he wanted. Solomon didn't ask for long life, riches, or the death of his enemies. Instead, he asked for wisdom so he could govern God's people properly. God was pleased with Solomon's request. Because of his selflessness, God not only gave Solomon what he asked for, but He also gave him riches and honor. It took all of 1 Kings 4 to list all that God blessed Solomon with – the number of officials, his daily provision, wealth, and how much wisdom he had.

When you pray for something with a pure heart and pure intentions, God doesn't just answer it in mediocracy; He answers with abundance. He goes beyond your expectations. God is the Creator of the world, but many people don't seem to grasp that understanding. If God can create something out of nothing; if God can breathe life into something dead; if God can create a human out of dirt; if God can turn dry bones into a living human again, how much more can God do for you? Stop putting limitations on such a big God! The Bible says come boldly before the throne of grace (Hebrews 4:16). It's okay to make your request known to your Father. He already knows what you need and what your heart desires; He's just waiting for you to ask. God can do exceedingly abundantly above all that you ask or think, according to the power that works in you (Ephesians 3:20). The best part is, as a son or daughter of God, you do not have to come from a place of begging. Just like you would ask your natural parent for something so effortlessly, you can do the same thing with God. He is your Abba Father. He loves you and wants to take care of you and bless you beyond your wildest dreams. What are you praying and believing God for?

REFLECTION

What are you praying and believing God for this week? Whether you need clarity, healing, a new job or promotion, or a breakthrough, go to God in prayer about it. Nothing is too big or small for Him. Faith is the foundation of your beliefs. If you know God is real, why is it so hard to have faith and believe God for what He can do? Write what you are believing God for. Spend time every day this week seeking God concerning your prayer request. Sit in His presence waiting and listening for an answer.

Sometimes, God will answer immediately. Sometimes, He will say no. Other times, He will say wait. God can speak in many ways. Don't put limitations or expectations on God's voice based on how you want to hear from Him. Use the space below to write down your prayer request, God's response, and how it manifested, if at all. Maybe you'll get a response in the immediate future, maybe next week or next month. It's okay to come back to write the response.

Week 32

FROM MOUTHPIECE TO HIGH PRIEST

But Moses pleaded with the Lord, "O Lord, I'm not very good with words. I never have been, and I'm not now, even though you have spoken to me. I get tongue-tied, and my words get tangled." Then the Lord asked Moses, "Who makes a person's mouth? Who decides whether people speak or do not speak, hear or do not hear, see or do not see? Is it not I, the Lord? Now go! I will be with you as you speak, and I will instruct you in what to say." But Moses again pleaded, "Lord, please! Send anyone else." Then the Lord became angry with Moses. "All right," he said. "What about your brother, Aaron the Levite? I know he speaks well. And look! He is on his way to meet you now. He will be delighted to see you. Talk to him, and put the words in his mouth. I will be with both of you as you speak, and I will instruct you both in what to do."
~~Exodus 4:10-15 NLT~~

"But you and your sons, the priests, must personally handle all the priestly rituals associated with the altar and with everything behind the inner curtain. I am giving you the priesthood as your special privilege of service. Any unauthorized person who comes too near the sanctuary will be put to death." The Lord gave these further instructions to Aaron: "I myself have put you in charge of all the holy offerings that are brought to me by the people of Israel. I have given all these consecrated offerings to you and your sons as your permanent share."
~~Numbers 18:7-8 NLT~~

If Moses had not used his inability to speak properly as an excuse, we probably wouldn't have known about Aaron, or he may not have shown up until later on in the Bible. Moses' speech caused Aaron to reap favor, blessings, and promotion. Aaron was faithful, diligent, and loyal to his brother and his assignment. He never complained or cared about being in the spotlight, and he didn't do it to gain anything in return. It wasn't until years later (Numbers 17 and 18) when God promoted Aaron. He went from mouthpiece to high priest! Not only that, but he was also the *first* high priest of the Israelites.

You may not understand why God has you where you are but believe that He has something greater in store for you. "Work willingly at whatever you do, as though you were working for the Lord rather than for people (Colossians 3:23 NLT). Whether at work, school, or church, serve faithfully, without complaint, and with a pure heart. What you plant in your "mouthpiece" season will determine what kind of harvest you will reap. You're about to go from "mouthpiece" to "high priest." Many of you are about to be the first! Your season of promotion is coming!

REFLECTION

This week's prayer:

Father, I ask that You give me wisdom to steward well over everything You have trusted me with - my family, friends, church, skills and talents, connections, time, finances, and work. Forgive me for all the times I saw myself as "less than" and inadequate. Forgive me for making excuses for why I couldn't do something. I appreciate everything You have done for me, and I do not take anything for granted. You have equipped me with everything I need to serve Your Kingdom well. I will use my gifts and talents for Your glory. I am important and needed in the body of Christ and in the marketplace. You have created me for a greater purpose, and even though it may overwhelm me, I trust You. I commit this day to serve You with humility, diligence, and a pure heart. In Jesus' name, amen.

This week's declarations:

I am enough. I am important. I am needed. I am gifted and talented. I am adequate and equipped to do the will of the Father. God has great plans for me, and I will walk in purpose. I have everything I need to fulfill God's plans and purpose for my life. I have favor with God and with man. I have wisdom to steward well over everything God has given me. I will not make excuses. I am righteous, therefore, I am bold as a lion! Everything I do, I do for the Lord. My season of promotion is coming!

HERE I AM!

Also I heard the voice of the Lord, saying: "Whom shall I send?
And who will go for Us?" Then I said, "Here am I! Send me."
~~Isaiah 6:8 NKJV~~

Notice the exclamation in Isaiah's response. He said, "Here am I!" Isaiah could not contain his excitement. He was eager to serve the Lord. Notice that God *did not* say what the assignment was first. It wasn't until *after* Isaiah said, "Send me" that God said, "Go, and tell this people: 'Keep on hearing, but do not understand; Keep on seeing, but do not perceive.' "Make the heart of this people dull, and their ears heavy, and shut their eyes; lest they see with their eyes, and hear with their ears, and understand with their heart, and return and be healed" (Isaiah 6:9-10 NKJV).

This was not an easy word to deliver, but Isaiah then asked the Lord, "how long?" He didn't try to back out of it; he didn't complain; he didn't question God's choice of person. He didn't say, "Wait, Lord, let me fast and pray about it first." Isaiah didn't care. He was waiting in expectation for God to use him because he saw it as an honor to serve the Lord and do His work.

"Here I am" is translated from the Hebrew word *hineni*. "It is mostly used when God personally calls on someone to do something difficult and important. It implies that a person is ready, willing, and able. "Here I am" has an even deeper meaning. It also means, here I stand. "Here I stand. It's not a meek thought; it's a bottom line. "Here I stand. Here I will make my stand. I know what will most likely happen, but it does not matter, since I will not be moving. This is where I am going to make my stand. Hineni." [6]

How many times have you prayed, "send me, Lord" or "use me, Lord."? Now that you have a better understanding of what "here I am" means, do you have a sincere hineni in your heart? When the opportunity arises, will you rise up and say, "here I am" without hesitating or knowing the assignment first? Will you say, "yes Lord, I am willing to go no matter the cost"? Jesus is looking for a willing heart. Eagerly wait in expectation.

REFLECTION

This week's prayer:

God, I want to do Your will. I want to say yes, but sometimes, I let fear, insecurities, and the opinions of people get in my way. I ask that You free me from everything that is hindering me from doing Your will, and give me the strength to say yes. I pray that You forgive me for all the times I said no out of fear. Forgive me for all the times I let opportunities slip away from me because I was concerned about what other people may think. I am good enough and strong enough to do what You have destined for me. I have a purpose to fulfill. I am able and willing because I can do all things through Christ who strengthens me. There is nothing more that I want than to please You. Help me recognize when opportunities are presented before me. I renew my yes to You today. God, I am ready. Choose me. Here I am. In Jesus' name, amen.

This week's declarations:

I can do all things through Christ who strengthens me. I am bold as a lion. I am good enough. I am strong enough. I have a purpose and I am going to fulfill it. Fear does not control me. I do not let people's opinions control me. I will give God my yes. I am willing, able, and ready for God to use me.

Week 34

ACTIVATE THE PROMISE OF GOD

After Lot had gone, the Lord said to Abram, "Look as far as you can
see in every direction— north and south, east and west. I am giving
all this land, as far as you can see, to you and your descendants as
a permanent possession. And I will give you so many descendants
that, like the dust of the earth, they cannot be counted! Go and walk
through the land in every direction, for I am giving it to you."
~~Genesis 13:14-17 NLT~~

In Genesis 13:17, God gave Abram instructions. He told Abram to go and walk
through the land in every direction. Abram had to walk in obedience and perform
this act of faith to activate the promise of God.

Promises of God require an act of faith. Sometimes people wait for God to do
all the work as if He is going to just drop the promise in their laps. Just because
God promised something, doesn't mean it's magically going to manifest. That's
like God promising to bless you with a better job but you don't apply for any
jobs. It's like God promising you a full ride to school, but you don't apply for any
scholarships, grants, or fellowships. It's like God promising to bless the business
you want to birth but you don't write out your business plan or research what you
need to do to get started.

Promises of God usually require you to put in the work. It requires you to go
somewhere, do something, or talk to someone. You have to take initiative and step
out on faith. Even if it doesn't make sense, God knows what's on the other side of
your obedience. He sees your effort and will bless the work of your hands. He has
already established connections to people, places, and things that will push you
further into your purpose. What promises are you holding on to? What promises
are you waiting to see come to past? Maybe God is waiting on you to walk in faith
to activate the promises He has for you. It is time for you to go, step out on faith,
and activate the promises of God in your life!

REFLECTION

What promises have God made you that you are still waiting to come to past? For each one, write what steps you can take to activate the promise. Afterall, faith without works is dead (James 2:26 NKJV).

1.

_____

_____

_____

_____

_____

_____

_____

2.

_____

_____

_____

_____

_____

_____

_____

3.

_____

_____

_____

_____

_____

_____

_____

Week 35

LOVING YOUR ENEMIES

The Lord said, "Go over to Straight Street, to the house of Judas. When you get there, ask for a man from Tarsus named Saul. He is praying to me right now. I have shown him a vision of a man named Ananias coming in and laying hands on him so he can see again." "But Lord," exclaimed Ananias, "I've heard many people talk about the terrible things this man has done to the believers in Jerusalem! And he is authorized by the leading priests to arrest everyone who calls upon your name." But the Lord said, "Go, for Saul is my chosen instrument to take my message to the Gentiles and to kings, as well as to the people of Israel. And I will show him how much he must suffer for my name's sake."
~~Acts 9:11-15 NLT~~

Remember when Apostle Paul went by his dual name, Saul, when he was a Pharisee? Although he had a life-changing experience, his encounter left him blind for three days.

God spoke to Ananias and told him to lay hands on Saul so he could see again. Ananias was so quick to object God's instructions. He didn't even know Saul personally, but he already saw him as an enemy because of all of the terrible things he heard about Saul. Ananias couldn't believe what God was asking him to do. However, God had great plans for Saul; God called him His chosen vessel!

Loving your enemies may be hard but that is what God has called you to do. Remember, your battle is not with flesh and blood, but the spirit(s) that are working within them. Your enemies don't hate you; they hate the Spirit that is in you. However, you never know what God is doing behind the scenes. Saul's life literally changed in a moment. One minute he was on his way to get papers signed to have believers arrested, and the next, he had an encounter with Jesus who called him His own and gave him an assignment. You never know what God is doing in the lives of those who persecute you.

Maybe a coworker goes out of their way to make your work environment difficult. You feel uncomfortable when you're around them and the sound of their voice makes you cringe. But what if one day, they came to work excited about their new salvation? Would you be guarded or celebrate with them? Who has God called you to love that seems difficult? Who is He asking you to pray for? Who is He asking you to smile and speak to despite how they treat you? It may be hard but press through the hate and love your enemies through the hardship and pain. You never know what God can do in a moment. Don't miss it!

REFLECTION

This week, make a conscious effort to go out of your way to show love to your enemy. Is there someone in your life who you do not like? Is there someone you go out of your way to avoid? Does the sound of their name boil you? Maybe there is someone in your life who actually hates you. Whoever that person is, show them the love of Christ. Buy them coffee. Hold the door open for them. Ask them how their day is going with a smile on your face and actually mean it and listen. If you see them struggling, offer a helping hand. They may ignore or reject you but keep trying. Keep showing love.

Who did you show love to this week? In what ways did you show love to that person? How did you feel showing love to that person? How did he/she respond? How did their response make you feel? Did you experience a breakthrough with the person?

_____

_____

_____

_____

_____

_____

_____

_____

_____

_____

_____

_____

_____

_____

_____

_____

_____

_____

_____

Week 36

HIDING FROM GOD

So Samuel brought all the tribes of Israel before the Lord, and the tribe of
Benjamin was chosen by lot. Then he brought each family of the tribe of
Benjamin before the Lord, and the family of the Matrites was chosen. And
finally Saul son of Kish was chosen from among them. But when they looked
for him, he had disappeared! So they asked the Lord, "Where is he?" And the
Lord replied, "He is hiding among the baggage." So they found him and brought
him out, and he stood head and shoulders above anyone else. Then Samuel
said to all the people, "This is the man the Lord has chosen as your king. No
one in all Israel is like him! And all the people shouted, "Long live the king!"
~~1 Samuel 10: 20-24 NLT~~

Prior to 1 Samuel 10, the Israelites were living solely by the guidance of the Lord.
They were the only group of people who were not ruled by a king. However, in 1
Samuel 8:5, the Israelites went to Samuel and said, "Give us a king to judge us like
all the other nations have" (NLT). Their request displeased Samuel because they
were rejecting God. The Lord told Samuel to give the Israelites what they wanted
because of their constant disobedience and rebellion. When Saul was chosen to be
their king, he ran away and hid among some baggage. However, the Lord revealed
Saul's location when the people inquired of him.

Saul was not the only one who attempted to hide or run away from God. Adam
and Eve hid from God after eating the fruit from the tree of knowledge of good
and evil. Jonah ran away when God instructed him to go to Nineveh and proclaim
judgement against the people. In all three of these examples, we can see that none
of them were successful in their attempt to hide or run away from God. Hebrews
4:13 (NLT) says, "Nothing in all creation is hidden from God. Everything is naked
and exposed before his eyes, and he is the one whom we are accountable."

How many times have God told you to do something that you didn't want to do
because the responsibility was too big? How many times did you run away or hide
from the purposes of God? How many of those times were successful? How many
of those times resulted in unnecessary warfare because of your disobedience?
God's will for your life will be done regardless of how many times you protest,
throw a temper tantrum, or delay. God's purpose for your life was established
before you were even born. You are already equipped with everything you need to
fulfill your purpose. Be confident in this, "that He who has begun a good work in
you will complete it until the day of Jesus Christ" (Philippians 1:6 NKJV). What
are you running away or hiding from now? Stop running. Come out of hiding.
It's time to go forth and do all that God called you to do. The world needs you!

REFLECTION

This week's prayer:

God, thank You for calling me Your chosen vessel to fulfill the purposes You have for me. I repent for running away and hiding from my calling. Forgive me for living a life of fear and not trusting You. I know You have called me to do great things on the earth. Thank You for giving me another day and another chance to do what You have called me to do. Let Your will be done in my life on earth as it is in heaven. My life is not my own and I say yes to Your will. I trust You to guide me every step of the way. Let Your name be glorified in everything I do. I lay down my will for Yours. When I do not have all the answers, reveal them to me. When I need confirmation, show me what to do next. When I need resources, connect me to the right people. When I need finances, make provision for Your Word says You give seed to the sower. Your ways are higher than my ways and Your thoughts are higher than my thoughts. You know what's best for me even when I think I'm making the right decision for my life. Align my will with Yours. In Jesus' name I pray, amen.

What is something you are running away or hiding from? Examine your heart and be honest with yourself and God. Why are you running or hiding? What are you afraid of? What is stopping you from doing what God has called you to do? Release it to God and trust Him.

Week 37

DON'T MISS IT

When Jesus caught sight of the city, he burst into tears with uncontrollable weeping over Jerusalem saying, "If only you could recognize that this day peace is within your reach! But you cannot see it. For the day is soon coming when your enemies will surround you, hem you in on every side, and lay siege to you. They will crush you to pieces, and your children too! And they will leave your city totally destroyed. Since you would not recognize God's day of visitation, you will see your day of devastation!"
~~Luke 19:41-44 TPT~~

There are only two recorded instances when Jesus wept in the Bible. The first occurred in the above scripture, and the second occurred when Jesus wept over the death of his friend Lazarus in John 11:35. In one instance, the depth of Jesus' pain was a result of a loss of a personal friendship. While the other was an expression of compassion for the city He loved so much because they were about to experience great destruction. Jesus saw the devastation that was to come upon Jerusalem due to their sin. Their rebellion and lack of trust blinded them from walking in the peace of God. The Israelites were God's chosen people – His beloved and the apple of His eye. However, they missed Him time and time again. Their sin distracted them and caused them to miss a divine visitation from God. As a result, they did not experience His protection from their enemies.

Had the Israelites stayed focused on and connected to God and interceded for themselves, their enemies would not have been able to overtake them, and they would not have been swallowed up by their situation. Just like the Israelites, people tend to focus more on their circumstances instead of focusing on the One who can bring them peace and cause an immediate shift. Don't miss your divine encounter and visitation from the Lord because you've allowed your circumstances or your sin to distract you. "Behold, the Lord's hand is not shortened, that it cannot save; nor His ear heavy, that it cannot hear" (Isaiah 49:1 NKJV). The Lord weeps over you and your situation. He doesn't like to see His children hurting or going through tough times. He sees your tears and hears your prayers. His hand is not out of reach. His touch reassures. His arms comfort. His love gives you peace. Like Jesus said to Jerusalem, if only you knew … if only you knew that peace is within your reach! Jesus' death and resurrection not only gifted you with the Holy Spirit but gave you direct access to the Father. It will not always be like this. Don't give up. Don't get discouraged. Don't lose focus that you miss a visitation from God. Keep pressing. Keep persevering. Keep holding on. Even if you cannot see it now, you will get through this. Grab ahold of His peace.

REFLECTION

This week's prayer:

Father, I pray that I will not be like the Israelites who were consumed and distracted by their circumstances and sin. The last thing I want to do is miss a visitation or even a moment with You. Help me to stay focused and connected to You. Surround me with the walls of Your salvation. I will keep my mind stayed on You because I trust You. Keep me in perfect peace. Smooth out the path ahead of me. I will show my trust in You by obeying Your Word. My heart's desire is to glorify Your name. Stretch out Your hand in my time of need. You have made a covenant of peace with me, which You said will never be removed. Let it extend to me in abundance like a river. Open my ears so I can hear and open my eyes so I can see that I may recognize Your day of visitation. In Jesus' name, amen.

This week really seek after and lean into the presence of God. Ask Him to make you sensitive to His presence and aware of His voice. God desires to speak to you just as much as you speak to Him. Whether it's a subtle still small voice or a full conversation, give God room to talk, and write down what He says.

_____

_____

_____

_____

_____

_____

_____

_____

_____

_____

_____

_____

_____

_____

_____

_____

_____

_____

Week 38

OBEDIENCE IN YOUR SACRIFICE

Some time later, God tested Abraham's faith. "Abraham!" God called.
"Yes," he replied. "Here I am." "Take your son, your only son – yes, Isaac,
whom you love so much – and go to the land of Moriah. Go and sacrifice
him as a burnt offering on one of the mountains, which I will show you."
~~Genesis 22:1-2 NLT~~

We all know the story of Abraham, but just in case some of you don't, let me give you the backstory. Abraham and his wife Sarah were barren and could not have children. God appeared to Abraham when he was 99 years old promising him that he will be a father of many nations, and even though Sarah was 90 years old, the promise would be fulfilled through her womb. God also told Abraham to name their son Isaac, which he did. We do not know how old Isaac was when God told Abraham to sacrifice him, but Isaac was the son of a covenant, and now, God was telling Abraham to offer him as a burn offering. Because of Abraham's willingness to be obedient, God stepped in at the last minute and provided a ram to be sacrificed instead. This was a story of faith, commitment, and obedience.

What if God told you to sacrifice or let go of something He promised you? How many of you would question whether God was really asking you to do such a thing? You would start rebuking Satan and saying things like, "the devil is a liar." You think, "there is absolutely no way God would tell me to sacrifice the blessing He gave me, Himself." Your blessing then becomes an idol because you refuse to let it go. But what you fail to realize is that in your obedience (even if it hurts to let it go), that God has something greater and better for you. However, your hand is closed so tight holding onto the old blessing that there is no room to receive the new blessing. You then become stagnant and start to mourn or hate the very thing you once loved, resulting in resentment towards the Father because of your lack of obedience. Letting go becomes your testimony because there is always more. There are more promotions, promises, opportunities, open doors, growth, and relationships. God has something greater and better for you. So right now, in this moment, if God has told you to let something go, do it. No more delay. If you don't have something to let go of now, remember this the next time God ask you to sacrifice or let go of something. Don't be so quick to rebuke Satan but lean into the voice of the Father. Trust Him and be obedient because there is another blessing after the sacrifice.

REFLECTION

What is God telling you to sacrifice, lay down, give up, or let go of? Why haven't you been obedient? Have you noticed challenges or hardships because of your delay? Write down the thing God told you to sacrifice and why you haven't let it go yet. Write down the consequences that resulted in you holding on to it. Then come back to this space a week, month, or even a year from now, and write what happened as a result of your obedience.

If you recently had to let go of something, how did it make you feel and what was the outcome? If you had to sacrifice something a while ago, write down your experience and the results of your obedience. Then when you are faced with a challenge of letting something else go, come back to this space as a reminder to trust God and the beauty of your obedience.

_____

_____

_____

_____

_____

_____

_____

_____

_____

_____

_____

_____

_____

_____

_____

_____

_____

_____

_____

_____

_____

Week 39

LAYING DOWN YOUR LIFE

At this they wept aloud again. Then Orpah kissed her mother-in-law goodbye,
but Ruth clung to her. "Look," said Naomi, "your sister-in-law is going back
to her people and her gods. Go back with her." But Ruth replied, "Don't urge
me to leave you or to turn back from you. Where you go I will go, and where
you stay I will stay. Your people will be my people and your God my God.
Where you die I will die, and there I will be buried. May the Lord deal with
me, be it ever so severely, if even death separates you and me." When Naomi
realized that Ruth was determined to go with her, she stopped urging her.
~~Ruth 1:14-18 NIV~~

To give some background information, Naomi had two sons who married Orpah
and Ruth. Both of her sons died, leaving their wives with their mother, Naomi.
There was a famine in the land, so Naomi decided to go back to her homeland,
Judah, with her daughters-in-law. As they were on their way, Naomi urged Orpah
and Ruth to go back to their mothers' houses. Orpah and Ruth then wept, refusing
to depart from Naomi. Their willingness to sacrifice everything they knew to be
with Naomi showed how deeply they loved and cared for her. However, Naomi
knew the sacrifices they would have to make, and she didn't want to be selfish.
Once again, Orpah and Ruth wept. This time, however, Orpah kissed Naomi
goodbye and left. Ruth, on the other hand, clung to Naomi, refusing to leave her
side.

We can compare this passage to having a relationship with God. Both women
loved Naomi and wept at the thought of being separated from her. However, after
much consideration and counting the cost, Orpah realized the price of laying
down her life to follow Naomi was too high. Ruth, however, was willing to give
up everything she knew to follow Naomi. She realized she would have to adapt to
a new culture. She realized she would have to be the sole provider for herself and
Naomi, and the possibility of facing economic hardship, but she didn't care. Ruth
was willing to lay down her life and follow Naomi at any cost. She made a vow
that she would only depart from Naomi by death. There was a sense of humility,
honor, and respect Ruth had for Naomi.

When things get tough, will you be like Orpah and stray away from God (stop reading the Bible, stop praying, stop fasting) or will you be like Ruth and *cling* to your Abba Father? How would you respond to a situation that shakes your faith? Will you hold on to your integrity, honor, loyalty, and respect? You say you would lay down your life for God. You say you would do *anything* for His glory. You want to be used by God and say things like, "I surrender. Your will, Lord, not mine" but do you really mean it? There will be times when you will be challenged, your faith will be shaken, or you will be faced with difficult situations. You may not always feel like walking in boldness or integrity. You may even experience moments of fear, doubt, and discomfort, but despite what may come your way, are you willing to lay down your life and continue to give God your yes?

REFLECTION

As you go through this week, think about difficult situations or challenges you may have faced. How did you respond? Did you remain humble and full of integrity? You can also reflect on your time/conversations with God. Did He tell you to do something that shook you, made you uncomfortable, or stopped you in your tracks? What reservations did you have? Why did you have that response? What can you do differently, if anything?

_____

_____

_____

_____

_____

_____

_____

_____

_____

_____

_____

_____

_____

_____

_____

_____

_____

_____

_____

_____

_____

_____

_____

Week 40

GOD IS WITH YOU

After the death of Moses the Lord's servant, the Lord spoke to
Joshua son of Nun, Moses' assistant. He said, "Moses my servant is
dead. Therefore, the time has come for you to lead these people, the
Israelites, across the Jordan River into the land I am giving them."
~~Joshua 1:1-2 NLT~~

Be strong and courageous, for you are the one who will lead these people
to possess all the land I swore to their ancestors I would give them. "Be
strong and very courageous. Be careful to obey all the instructions Moses
gave you. Do not deviate from them, turning either to the right or to the
left. Then you will be successful in everything you do. "Study this Book
of Instruction continually. Meditate on it day and night so you will be sure
to obey everything written in it. Only then will you prosper and succeed
in all you do. This is my command– be strong and courageous! Do not be
afraid or discouraged. For the Lord your God is with you wherever you go.
~~Joshua 1:6-9 NLT~~

In Joshua chapter one, God made Joshua the leader of Israel. He was to lead the
Israelites across the Jordan River into the Promised Land. One thing that is really
encouraging is the fact that Joshua did not overthink the situation. As soon as
God gave him instruction, Joshua went straight to work, taking charge over the
Israelites.

Sometimes we compromise God's plan for our lives because we overthink or
allow fear to hinder us from moving forward. So many things went wrong in
the wilderness during Moses' reign over the Israelites due to their disobedience.
There were so many scenarios that could have paralyzed Joshua from taking his
place as their leader. He could have denied the role because he didn't want to
take on the responsibility of leading such a rebellious group of people. Maybe
he was going to die in the wilderness like Moses did. He could've worried about
what would've happened once they crossed the Jordan River. Joshua was aware
that there were multiple descendants of people already living in the Promised
Land. How was he going to defeat the Canaanites, Hittites, Hivites, Perizzites,
Girgashites, Amorites, and Jebusites?

Had Joshua had this mindset, he would have allowed fear to paralyze him, jeopardizing himself from being the great leader God called him to be. We do not know what was going through Joshua's mind while God was giving him instructions, but God knew. So much so that God saw fit to tell Joshua to be strong and courageous *three* times! God made a promise to never to leave nor forsake Joshua and that He was going to be with him wherever he went. With these words, Joshua confidently led the Israelites across the Jordan River, conquered the land, and entered the Promised Land. Like Joshua, God will never leave you nor forsake you. He is with you wherever you go. Go forth!

REFLECTION

Did God tell you to do something but you allowed fear to paralyze you? I want to encourage you to step out in faith. Apply for that job, start that book, write out that business plan, etc. Whatever it is, step out in faith and trust God to do the rest. Do not be afraid but be strong and of good courage for God is with you wherever you go. He will not leave you nor forsake you!

This week's prayer:
Father, You know the plans You have for me. Your plans for my life are to prosper me and not harm me. Your plans give me a hope and a future, therefore, I will put my trust in You. Your thoughts are not my thoughts and Your ways are higher than my ways. You know what's best for me. Give me ears to hear and eyes to see Your truth. Let wisdom and discernment be my potion so that I will not turn to the right or left, but remain focus on my purpose. Holy Spirit, guide my ways and establish the work of my hands so that I will be successful in everything I do. I will be strong and of good courage because You are with me wherever I go. I will not be afraid or discouraged because You will never leave me nor forsake me.

This week's declaration:
I will not allow fear to paralyze me. I will walk in obedience and do whatever the Lord asks of me. I will step out in faith and trust God to do the rest. I am not fearful. I am strong and very courageous. I will be successful in everything I do because the Lord is with me wherever I go and He will not leave me nor forsake me.

At the end of the week, use the space below to record your progress. Journal your wins, victories, struggles, and testimonies. If things didn't go as you may have wanted, what could you have done differently and how can you respond next time?

_____

_____

_____

_____

_____

_____

_____

_____

_____

Week 41

PURPOSE IN YOUR PAIN

When Mary arrived and saw Jesus, she fell at his feet and said, "Lord, if only you had been here, my brother would not have died." When Jesus saw her weeping and saw the other people wailing with her, a deep anger welled up within him, and he was deeply troubled. "Where have you put him?" he asked them. They told him, "Lord, come and see." Then Jesus wept. The people who were standing nearby said, "See how much he loved him!"
~~John 11:32-36 NLT~~

John 11 is a passage of three siblings, Mary, Martha, and Lazarus. Mary and Martha sent a message to Jesus informing Him that His friend, Lazarus, was sick. By the time Jesus arrived to Bethany, their hometown, Lazarus had already been in his grave for four days. Jesus purposely waited until Lazarus was dead before arriving so He could perform a miracle and strengthen the faith of those who were present. In Mary's distress, she blamed Jesus for her brother's death. When Jesus saw Mary and the others weeping, Jesus became angry and wept with them. He then went into Lazarus' grave, prayed, and commanded Lazarus to come out. At that moment, Lazarus rose from the dead and the people unwrapped his body.

Jesus knew Lazarus was sick before He even received the message regarding his illness, but He also knew that Lazarus' sickness was not going to end in death. Jesus knew He was going to heal Lazarus – not because they were close friends (verse 3), but in order for God to get the glory. Because of the love Jesus had for them, He was greatly troubled and wept. That is how God reacts when you are hurting and in pain. You may not know the end result, but God does. God exists outside of time and knows your beginning to your end. Jesus could have healed Lazarus immediately just by speaking a word, but there was a greater purpose. You may wonder why you're going through the things you're going through. You may wonder where God is in the mist of your pain, but He is right there with you. Psalms 56:8 (NLT) says, "You keep track of all my sorrows. You have collected all my tears in your bottle. You have recorded each one in your book." God has not forgotten about you. Just like Lazarus' death brought glory to God, so will your situation. Your pain will get others through their time of trouble. Your testimony will encourage others and give them strength and hope. It may not seem like it now, but God will be glorified in your situation so you can praise the One who brought you out. What you are going through won't last forever. There is a greater purpose in your pain and God is going to heal you from your sorrow so He can get the glory. Holy Spirit is the great Comforter. Rest and find strength in Him.

REFLECTION

Sometimes the best form of healing is release. Keeping all of that sadness or frustration built up inside of you can affect your physical and mental health. Use the space below to pour your heart out to God. Psalms 55:22 (AMPC) says, "Cast your burden on the Lord [releasing the weight of it] and He will sustain you; He will never allow the [consistently] righteous to be moved (made to slip, fall, or fail)." Nothing you share with the Lord will throw Him off guard or upset Him. Release the weight of your burden to the Lord.

Week 42

VICTORIOUS

I know all the things you do. I have seen your hard work and your
patient endurance. I know you don't tolerate evil people. You have
examined the claims of those who say they are apostles but are not.
You have discovered they are liars. You have patiently suffered for me
without quitting. Anyone with ears to hear must listen to the Spirit
and understand what he is saying to the churches. To everyone who is
victorious I will give fruit from the tree of life in the paradise of God.
~~Revelations 2:2-3, 7 NLT~~

God knew everything the church of Ephesus did. He saw their hard work and their
patient endurance. God saw how they patiently suffered for Him without quitting.
But He also saw their sin and gave them room to repent. Here is the thing – life is
going to be hard and knock you down. You are going to mess up. You are going to
sin. You are going to have ungodly thoughts. Even Apostle Paul said in Romans
7:15 (TPT), "I'm a mystery to myself, for I want to do what is right, but end up
doing what my moral instincts condemn." You are human and you are not perfect.
But that does not stop God from loving you. God is not like man. His love does not
compare to any human love that you give or receive on earth. His love is perfect.
His love is everlasting. His love is unconditional. Nothing *you do* can separate
you from the love of God (Romans 8:38).

If you find yourself running from the Father's presence or you have not spent time
worshiping Him or reading the Bible because of your guilt and shame, it is not too
late to run back into the arms of the Father. "So now there is no condemnation
for those who belong to Christ Jesus. And because you belong to him, the power
of the life-giving Spirit has freed you from the power of sin that leads to death"
(Romans 8:1-2 NLT). There is nothing you can do to earn God's love because
His love for you does not change. He wants to embrace you in His presence. You
don't have to do good deeds to prove your love to Him. There is nothing you can
do to make up for your sin. All you have to do is repent. The goal is to patiently
endure. The goal is not to quit when you are suffering for God. The goal is to be
victorious. You are an overcomer. Satan is already defeated. God has the keys to
the Kingdom. You are His son/daughter. You already won!

REFLECTION

This week's declarations:
I am not condemned. The power of Jesus freed me from sin. I will not quit. I am victorious. I will overcome every obstacle and trial that comes my way. Nothing that I do will separate me from the love of the Father. I am a son/daughter and His love for me is unconditional.

This week go deeper in your pursuit of God and record your experience.

_____

_____

_____

_____

_____

_____

_____

_____

_____

_____

_____

_____

_____

_____

_____

_____

_____

_____

_____

_____

_____

_____

_____

_____

Week 43

ACCUSATIONS AND ASSUMPTIONS

Look at me! Would I lie to your face? Stop assuming my
guilt, for I have done no wrong. Do you think I am lying?
Don't I know the difference between right and wrong?
~~Job 6:28-30 NLT~~

Shouldn't someone answer this torrent of words? Is a person proved
innocent just by a lot of talking? Should I remain silent while you babble
on? When you mock God, shouldn't someone make you ashamed? You
claim, 'My beliefs are pure,' and 'I am clean in the sight of God.' If only
God would speak; if only he would tell you what he thinks! If only he
would tell you the secrets of wisdom, for true wisdom is not a simple
matter. Listen! God is doubtless punishing you far less than you deserve!
~~Job 11:2-6 NLT~~

Job defended his righteousness even when his wife and friends doubted him.
They accused Job of being a sinful man resulting in God's wrath. However, God,
Himself, said there was no one like Job on earth. God knew Job was a blameless
and upright man who feared Him and turned away from evil (Job 1:8). God knew
Job was righteous when nobody else did. Job's friends knew that he was a man
of integrity, honor, loyalty, and compassion. However, none of that mattered.
Everything they knew about Job was thrown out the window. They looked at his
situation and assumed he was at fault. They didn't consider that Job was being
tested by God or if it was a spiritual attack. His friends automatically assumed he
was paying the price for his sins. Job did not receive encouragement or support
from the people he loved the most. Instead, he was accused, judged, and belittled.

You can be a God-fearing Christian living a righteous life, yet there will be
people who form negative assumptions about you. When you grow in Christ,
people will say, "you've changed." You no longer say, think, or do the things you
used to. Change can be uncomfortable to those around you because you don't fit
in their box anymore. However, they only get a glimpse of your life. They form
an image of who they want you to be and expect you to live up to their false
expectations. The only person you need to please is God. The more you grow,
tests and challenges will get harder. Don't let people discourage you and hinder
your growth. God will send the right people into your life who will understand,
encourage and support you, pray for you, keep you accountable, and bring more
peace than strife. Keep pursing God. Keep seeking His face. Keep pressing. Keep
pursing righteousness. In the end, it is God you have to stand before, not man.

REFLECTION

This week's prayer:
Father, thank You for Your unconditional love toward me. Thank You for always being there for me. Your Word says You will never leave me nor forsake me. When my loved ones abandon me, You will take care of me. You are my light and salvation. Whom shall I fear? You are the strength of my life. Whom shall I be afraid? In times of trouble, give me strength. You are my shield and strong tower. Hide me under the shadow of your wings. When people wrongly accuse me, bring to light what was conspired in darkness. Expose the lies and reveal the truth in my favor. Be my Defender, oh God, for I have never seen the righteous forsaken. I will prevail when darkness seems to close in. Help me to continue to live a blameless and righteous life. Let the fear of the Lord be my portion. I pray that when temptation comes my way, I will turn away from evil. Guard my thoughts and my mouth from evil. Give me peace of mind so I do not linger on false accusations. I trust that You will fight for me. Holy Spirit, I ask that You give me discernment and wisdom in how I should respond. I pray that I will always represent You well and live a life that is pleasing and acceptable in Your sight. I pray that I will not lose hope, get discouraged, or give up because my trust is in You. I pray that I will always seek after You and pursue righteousness. Let desperation for You burn within me so that I will always run to You in the good times and bad. Father, I ask that You reveal those who are against me and who have ill intentions towards me. Send people in my life who I can build genuine friendships with and grow together in Christ with. Help me to be just as genuine, kind, giving, supportive, and encouraging in my friendships as I want from others. In Jesus' name, amen.

This week's declarations:
I am blameless and righteous. I fear God and turn away from evil. I am a man/woman of integrity and honor. I am respectful, loyal, and compassionate. I will remain faithful and hopeful in times of trouble. I will not get discouraged or give up because my trust is in God. When darkness tries to overtake me, I will be a light on a hill that cannot be hidden. I will represent God well with my words and actions. I live to please God and not man. I am about my Father's business and I will do His will and walk in purpose. I will continue to seek God even when I feel alone. The version of me that people created is not my responsibility. I know who I am and whose I am. I am the son/daughter of the King – my Defender and Strong Tower. I will not be dismayed or afraid.

Week 44

MADE STRONG IN WEAKNESS

Each time he said, "My grace is all you need. My power works best in
weakness." So now I am glad to boast about my weaknesses, so that the
power of Christ can work through me. That's why I take pleasure in my
weaknesses, and in the insults, hardships, persecutions, and troubles
that I suffer for Christ. For when I am weak, then I am strong.
~~2 Corinthian 12:9-10 NLT~~

How many of you can say that you take pleasure when you are insulted and have
to endure hardships and persecution? How many of you would happily boast in
your weaknesses in times of trouble? Imagine having this conversation: "My
supervisor has been giving me so much grief lately. Today, I was even called
incompetent. God's grace overwhelmed me and His power made me so strong
in that moment." Most people would not respond in that manner. How about as a
parent? Have you ever dealt with a rebellious teenager? "My child is hanging out
with the wrong crowd, won't listen, refuses to go to church, goes to parties all
hours of the night, and constantly has an attitude. I take pleasure in this situation!"
Realistically, in moments like these, parents are grieved over their children and are
warring in prayer for their salvation. They are not going to their family and friends
boasting about the hardships they are facing. Yes, our trust is in God during times
of trouble, but not many people will boast about their weaknesses when they are
going through the process. Matter of fact, boasting usually comes after God has
brought them through their situation, and they have a testimony.

However, there is hope! In 2 Corinthians 12:9, the Lord told Apostle Paul, "My
grace is all you need. My power works best in weakness."

Grace is translated from the Greek word, *charis*, which means "That which affords
joy, pleasure, delight, sweetness, charm, loveliness; Good will, loving-kindness,
favor; The merciful kindness by which God, exerting his holy influence upon
souls, turns them to Christ, keeps, strengthens, increases them in Christian faith,
knowledge, affection, and kindles them to the exercise of the Christian virtues." [7]

It's the grace of God (joy, pleasure, loving-kindness, favor) that keeps, strengthens,
and increases you in faith, knowledge, and affection that gives you the ability to
exercise Christian virtues. That is all you need because God's power works best
in your time of weakness. This was how Apostle Paul was able to take pleasure
in his weakness and boast in his times of trouble. When you are weak, then God
will make you strong.

REFLECTION

This week, ask Holy Spirit to shift the way you think and respond to different situations. Ask Him to make you presently aware of those moments so that the power of Christ can work through you so you can exercise Christian virtues. Write down moments when God's strength was made perfect in your weakness. For when you are weak, then you are made strong.

_____

_____

_____

_____

_____

_____

_____

_____

_____

_____

_____

_____

_____

_____

_____

_____

_____

_____

_____

_____

_____

_____

_____

_____

_____

CONSULT WITH GOD

"What sorrow awaits my rebellious children," says the Lord. "You make plans that are contrary to mine. You make alliances not directed by my Spirit, thus piling up your sins. For without consulting me, you have gone down to Egypt for help. You have put your trust in Pharaoh's protection. You have tried to hide in his shade. But by trusting Pharaoh, you will be humiliated, and by depending on him, you will be disgraced. For though his power extends to Zoan and his officials have arrived in Hanes, all who trust in him will be ashamed. He will not help you. Instead, he will disgrace you." This message came to me concerning the animals in the Negev: The caravan moves slowly across the terrible desert to Egypt– donkeys weighed down with riches and camels loaded with treasure – all to pay for Egypt's protection. They travel through the wilderness, a place of lionesses and lions, a place where vipers and poisonous snakes live. All this, and Egypt will give you nothing in return.
~~Isaiah 30:1-6 NLT~~

When the Israelites were in trouble, they consulted amongst themselves and decided to go to Egypt to seek help. The Israelites were God's chosen people, His beloved children whom He had taken care of and protected time after time. However, they failed to seek and consult with the One who has never failed them. The Israelites made plans to run back to the people who once enslaved them. And for what? To be humiliated and disgraced and gain nothing in return. Their fear and anxiety clouded their judgment.

We live in a world where people love to share things with their family, friends, coworkers, and even strangers. People gossip, tell jokes, vent, grieve, boast, and ask for help. As humans, people take comfort in having a listening ear, especially during times of trouble. People want to feel secured, comforted, and protected. Nobody wants to go through hard times alone. But how often do you run into the arms of the Father before telling people your problems? How often do you sit in His presence waiting to be embraced or comforted? How often do you wait for God to answer you or give you a solution before seeking guidance from someone else?

Like the Israelites, sometimes, going to someone else can do more harm than good. For example, if you're going through financial hardship and decide to go to someone for help, they may lend you the money, but at what cost? You may go to someone in confidence and later discover that your business has been spread, causing humiliation, embarrassment, or disgrace. You didn't gain anything, but instead, it felt like you lost everything.

It's okay to share your heart with others but use discernment and wisdom. Stop running to people who can't do anything for you or have ill intentions towards you. Who are mere men that can save you better than God? Who are mere men that can provide for you better than God can? Remember to consult with the Lord first. He cares about every detail of your life.

REFLECTION

This week, be intentional about sharing your heart with God first. It can be something that seems small and insignificant or something major or exciting. Just go to Him first.

Day 1:

_____

_____

_____

_____

_____

Day 2:

_____

_____

_____

_____

Day 3:

_____

_____

_____

_____

Day 4:

_____

_____

_____

_____

Day 5:

_____

_____

_____

_____

_____

_____

Day 6:

_____

_____

_____

_____

_____

_____

Day 7:

_____

_____

_____

_____

_____

_____

Week 46

FORGIVEN AND ETERNALLY LOVED

Yet I still dare to hope when I remember this: The faithful love
of the Lord never ends! His mercies never cease. Great is his
faithfulness; his mercies begin afresh each morning. I say to myself,
"The Lord is my inheritance; therefore, I will hope in him!" The
Lord is good to those who depend on him, to those who search for
him. So it is good to wait quietly for salvation from the Lord.
~~Lamentations 3:21-26 NLT~~

In the book of Jeremiah, the Lord sent prophets to warn the Israelites about the
coming destruction if they did not repent. However, they did not listen. The downfall
of Jerusalem was fulfilled Lamentations. Despite the Israelites' hardship, they
remembered and honored the Lord. They knew what they did was wrong, and
although they suffered, they acknowledged God and had hope in Him. The Israelites
realized God's love for them never ended. Nothing they did stopped God from
loving them. The Israelites saw God's love, compassion, and forgiveness from
generation to generation. Even in the midst of hardship, they found their strength in
the Lord. Although the Israelites lost everything, they knew if they repented, God
would forgive them and restore the joy of their salvation.

As a Christian, you are not perfect and fall short of the glory of God. Whether
you sinned yesterday or even a few minutes ago, God's love for you doesn't
change. However, for some people, that's hard to believe. Their sin drowns them
in condemnation. They lose hope. They think they have to do good deeds in order
to be accepted by God again. But I have good news! That is a lie from the enemy.
You have been redeemed. All you have to do is repent. God wants nothing more
than to embrace you and draw you closer to Him. Jesus gave you a gift when He
died and resurrected, and that gift is eternal love. Have hope in this:

"Can anything ever separate us from Christ's love? Does it mean he no longer
loves us if we have trouble or calamity, or are persecuted, or hungry, or destitute,
or in danger, or threatened with death? (As the Scriptures say, "For your sake we
are killed every day; we are being slaughtered like sheep.") No, despite all these
things, overwhelming victory is ours through Christ, who loved us. And I am
convinced that nothing can ever separate us from God's love. Neither death nor
life, neither angels nor demons, neither our fears for today nor our worries about
tomorrow—not even the powers of hell can separate us from God's love. No power
in the sky above or in the earth below—indeed, nothing in all creation will ever
be able to separate us from the love of God that is revealed in Christ Jesus our
Lord" (Romans 8:35-39 NLT).

REFLECTION

This week's prayer:

Father, Your Word says that You will not allow me to be tempted beyond my ability to resist, and that You will provide a way of escape. So I ask, Father, that I will always choose the path that leads to righteousness. Forgive me for all the times that I have chosen to please the desires of my flesh. Let my desire to please You grow deeper every day. Your Word says there is no condemnation for those who are in Christ Jesus. Because of Your sacrifice, I am forgiven, redeemed, and set free. Your Word says out of the abundance of the heart the mouth speaks so I submit my heart and mind to You. Purify my heart and let my thoughts come under alignment with Your Word. Father, thank You for Your unconditional, unwavering, and never-ending love towards me. I thank You because nothing that I do will ever separate me from Your love. Great is Your faithfulness, oh God. Lord, my inheritance is in You, therefore, so is my hope. I will depend on You and search for You all the days of my life. I will dedicate my life to worshiping You, and You alone. You are my everything. In Jesus' name I pray, amen.

Use the space below to talk to God. You can confess your sins, pour out your heart, lay down your burdens, or spend time worshipping and praising God. Maybe you want to tell Him about your day – what was good, what went wrong, or what you could've done differently. Whatever it is, communicating with God develops your relationship with Him.

Week 47

CONTINUOUSLY INCREASING IN FAITH

For this very reason, make every effort to add to your faith excellence,
to excellence, knowledge; to knowledge, self-control; to self-control,
perseverance; to perseverance, godliness; to godliness, brotherly affection;
to brotherly affection, unselfish love. For if these things are really yours and
are continually increasing, they will keep you from becoming ineffective and
unproductive in your pursuit of knowing our Lord Jesus Christ more intimately.
But concerning the one who lacks such things– he is blind. That is to say, he
is nearsighted, since he has forgotten about the cleansing of his past sins.
~~2 Peter 1:5-9 NET~~

Building your faith is so important, and this scripture tells you how to develop it. The first is excellence. Operating in excellence does not mean perfection; it means doing your best wholeheartedly with pure intentions. Next is knowledge, which means to have insight and understanding. It is important that you have insight about what is going on around you, along with what is happening in the natural and spiritual realm so that you can be alert, discern the times, and know what to pray for. Then, self-control. Self-control prevents you from being impulsive with your actions and emotions. It causes you to think and make rational decisions.

Next, perseverance. Being a Christian isn't easy. It is important that you are persistent in your faith despite hardships. Godliness means to show reverence and respect. Finally, brotherly affection and unselfish love. Sometimes, loving people can be challenging when you don't even like them, but that is why you have to add *unselfish* love to your faith. When Jesus was asked what the greatest commandment is, He said love God first and love people (Matthew 22:37-39). God loved you when you were still a sinner, so it is important to show that same unselfish love that God gave you to those who are not yet in the faith.

Having these qualities prevent you from becoming ineffective and unproductive in your pursuit of knowing Jesus. Nothing compares to having an intimate relationship with Him. He is the foundation of your faith, and you cannot have a relationship with Him if you don't know Him intimately. When you have these qualities, your spiritual senses become more sensitive, which draws you closer to God. The lack thereof can result in spiritual blindless which can lead to a distant relationship with God and a life of rebellion. You do not have to develop these qualities one at a time; you continuously increase them simultaneously. These are things you can work on every single day. It doesn't just draw you closer to the Father, but it also gives you joy and a peace of mind.

REFLECTION

This week's declaration:
I operate in excellence in everything I do. I am knowledgeable and have self-control. I have the strength to persevere through anything because God is with me. I am a godly person. I show brotherly affection and unselfish love to everyone. I will not be ineffective and unproductive in my pursuit of knowing Jesus more intimately. I am growing in faith daily. I will not be blind and forget what Jesus did for me on the cross – my sins are cleansed.

Go through the qualities listed in 2 Peter 1:5-9 and figure out which one(s) you struggle with or need to improve. This week, ask Holy Spirit to make you aware of when you are not operating in these qualities in that moment. These qualities will affect how you think, talk, act, and respond. Record your progress in the space below.

_____

_____

_____

_____

_____

_____

_____

_____

_____

_____

_____

_____

_____

_____

_____

_____

_____

_____

Week 48

PEACE IN THE MIST OF CHAOS

Joshua then commanded the officers of Israel, "Go through the camp and tell the people to get their provisions ready. In three days you will cross the Jordan River and take possession of the land the Lord your God is giving you." Then Joshua called together the tribes of Reuben, Gad, and the half-tribe of Manasseh. He told them, "Remember what Moses, the servant of the Lord, commanded you: 'The Lord your God is giving you a place of rest. He has given you this land.' ~~Joshua 1:10-13 NLT~~

When Moses died in the wilderness, God appointed Joshua as the new leader. It was now Joshua's responsibility to lead this rebellious group of people who caused them to wander in the wilderness for 40 years into battle against seven different tribes. The Israelites struggled with trust and idolatry, and often times did their own thing resulting in chaos, lies, and confusion. How were they going to conquer the Canaanites, Hittites, Hivites, Perizzites, Girgashites, Amorites, and Jebusites? Joshua couldn't dwell on that. He had to focus on the mission, trust God, and be obedient. Notice that God didn't tell Joshua he was going to conquer the land of milk and honey, but instead, God said He was giving him a place of rest.

Despite the chaos surrounding you, you can take comfort in knowing that God is with you and will get you through it. Regardless of what may come your way, you can find rest in the Father because you know He will protect you, provide for you, comfort you, and bless you in the mist of your situation. It may not seem like it now, but God is not done with you yet. You have so much to live for and a purpose to fulfill. You have come too far to give up now. It may feel like you are in the middle of the wilderness in a barren land, but this will not last forever. God wants to bring you into a land filled with milk and honey. He wants to bring you into a place of rest and give you a life of prosperity, peace, favor, and blessings.

In Mark 4:35-41, Jesus and His disciples were on a boat when a fierce storm arose on the sea. The disciples panicked and woke Jesus up. He then commanded the winds and waves to be still and asked the disciples why they were afraid. When things around you go into havoc, you can be like Jesus and rest in the mist of the storm. You of little faith, why are you afraid? Why are you letting people get to you? Why are you giving power to your situation? God has given you authority to speak to your circumstances and command them to align with the will of God. You have no need to worry because God is with you. He is your Protector, Strong Tower, Fortress, and Provider. Your trust is in Him. He is your God, and you are the one that He loves. Rest in Him so you can find rest in the mist of the chaos.

REFLECTION

This week's prayer:

Father, I repent for allowing fear of the unknown to cloud my judgement and view of You. Father, during times of trouble, uncertainty, and chaos, give me rest. I ask that You give me strength to persevere so I can come out strong. Father, I ask that I won't just survive, but I will be victorious. I ask that You bless me in the midst of a barren land. I will find strength, peace, joy, and hope in You. Father, I trust You as my Provider, my Healer, my Strong Tower, my Deliverer, and my Protector. I take comfort in knowing that You are with me. Because I have breath in my body, I know You are not done with me and I have a purpose to fulfill. I will not give up. I thank You because You are bringing me out of the barren land into the land filled with milk and honey. You are bringing me into a place of rest that is full of peace, prosperity, joy, favor, and blessings. As You commanded the winds and waves to be still, I ask that You bring stillness to my situation. Strengthen my faith so I will not be afraid. Your Word says life and death is in the power of the tongue, so I speak life to my situation. When things spiral out of control, I will be like Jesus who was able to rest in the midst of the storm. Let everything in my life align with Your will. I will not let things around me distract me and take my focus off of You. Let Your will be done in my life on earth as it is in heaven. I release my worries, hopelessness, and fears to You and exchange it for Your peace, rest, and joy. In Jesus' name, amen.

Come back towards the end of the week and reflect on your prayers, declaration, quiet time, and worship. How did God move on your behalf this week? Was there a shift in your situation or your perspective? Did God give you revelation as to why you're going through this season? What have you learned about yourself? What areas of growth do you need to work on?

_____

_____

_____

_____

_____

_____

_____

_____

_____

Week 49

DISOBEDIENCE IN YOUR PURPOSE

The Lord gave this message to Jonah son of Amittai: "Get up and go to
the great city of Nineveh. Announce my judgment against it because I
have seen how wicked its people are." But Jonah got up and went in the
opposite direction to get away from the Lord. He went down to the port of
Joppa, where he found a ship leaving for Tarshish. He bought a ticket and
went on board, hoping to escape from the Lord by sailing to Tarshish.
~~Jonah 1:1-4 NLT~~

The Lord gave Jonah an assignment and he deliberately ran away to avoid doing
what God told him to do. As a result, God caused a violent storm to occur in the
sea, putting the lives of everyone on board at risk. The sailors threw Jonah into
the sea and the storm immediately ceased. Jonah was then swallowed by a great
fish where he stayed for three days and three nights.

Jonah blatantly disobeyed God, but one thing for sure, whether you're obedient
or not, God's will for your life will prevail. Your disobedience can not only
delay purpose, but it can also have a negative impact on those you are assigned
to and can cause unnecessary hardships for you and those around you. Because
of Jonah's disobedience, a violent storm broke out that could've killed everyone
on board. If Jonah never obeyed God, the people of Nineveh could have been
destroyed by God's wrath. When it comes to your purpose, your actions don't just
affect you but every person that is connected to your life.

When you disobey God and things don't go your way, you pout and complain as
if it was God's fault that put you in that situation. You start to question God or cry
out to Him to rescue you. Crying out to God is not an issue, but know that when
God brings you out, it is an exchange for your obedience, otherwise, you will end
up in a cycle of hardships.

The amazing thing is, God exist in and out of time. Nothing surprises God or
catches Him off guard. God knew Jonah was going to be disobedient, but He
arranged for a great fish to swallow him. Even in your disobedience, God will go
ahead of you and make arrangements on your behalf. Disobeying God is never
okay, but even in your disobedience, God will always be glorified. In the midst
of Jonah's disobedience, the sailors on the boat were so amazed at God's power
that they offered a sacrifice and vowed to serve Him.

God could have chosen anyone else to fulfill that assignment when Jonah decided to disobey Him, but God wanted Jonah to do it. Often times, we cry out for God to use us, but only on our terms when it doesn't inconvenience us or take us out of our comfort zone. Although we're all replaceable, there are certain assignments that God specifically created for you, and you are the only one who can complete it. No matter how many times you say no, run away, or ignore God's instructions, the will of God will always be fulfilled.

REFLECTION

Being obedient may seem scary sometimes, and can come with challenges, but it is always rewarding. Step out on faith and trust God. If God can trust you with little, He can trust you with much. It's time to repent and do what God told you to do.

This week's prayer:
Lord, forgive me for my disobedience. I repent for _____
. Forgive me for every person whose life was impacted by my decision to be disobedient. Even in this, I ask that Your name be glorified. Thank You for the redemption power of the blood of Jesus. Father, You could have chosen anyone but You chose me, and for that, I'm grateful. I lay down my life, my will, and my intentions, and I say yes to Your will. I will no longer run away or ignore You. Your plans for my life are far greater than I can think or imagine. Your plans are to prosper me and not harm me. You not only want what's best for me, but You have called me to make an impact. My life is not my own, so I surrender to Your will. Lord, I bind the spirit of fear and pride over my life, and I come against anything that is holding me back from moving forward in purpose. Father, You have given me authority to trample over the enemy. Whom shall I fear? Give me the courage and strength I need to do what You have called me to do. Holy Spirit, guide me and give me wisdom. I cannot do this on my own. I need You. Let there be a realignment in my life. Thank You for not giving up on me. I praise You because You are merciful and kind. Your love, Father, is eternal and unconditional. In Jesus' name, amen.

Revisit the last thing God told you to do that you ignored, ran away from, delayed, or said no to. What was it? What reason did you have for making that decision of disobedience? How has that affected you and the people around you? Lastly, what steps can you take to walk in obedience and do what God told you to do?

_____

_____

_____

_____

_____

_____

_____

_____

_____

_____

Week 50

COMFORTED SO YOU CAN COMFORT

He comforts us in all our troubles so that we can comfort others.
When we are troubled, we will be able to give them the same comfort
God has given us. For the more we suffer for Christ, the more God
will shower us with his comfort through Christ. Even when we are
weighed down with troubles, it is for your comfort and salvation!
For when we ourselves are comforted, we will certainly comfort
you. Then you can patiently endure the same things we suffer.
~~2 Corinthians 1:4-6 NLT~~

When you go through hard times, do you walk around with a sad look on your face
or have a woe is me attitude so you can get attention or sympathy? The Bible says
God comforts us in *all* our troubles so that we can comfort others. Before Jesus'
death, He told His disciples, "Nevertheless I tell you the truth; It is expedient for
you that I go away: for if I go not away, the Comforter will not come unto you; but
if I depart, I will send him unto you" (John 16:7 KJV). Jesus gave us the promise
of the Holy Spirit, our Comforter, who lives in us. Because the Holy Spirit lives
in us, we have access to immediate comfort.

Take comfort in this scripture: "Cast your burden on the Lord [release it] and He
will sustain and uphold you; He will never allow the righteous to be shaken (slip,
fall, fail)" (Psalms 55:22 AMP).

The more you suffer for Christ, the more God will *shower* you with His comfort.
Think about what happens when you get in the shower. Streams of water pour on
you. That is what God wants to do. He wants to pour His comfort on you so when
you are weighed down, you are not burdened. In return, you can then give those
who are suffering the same comfort God has given you.

There is absolutely *nothing* too big or too small for God to handle. Nothing
catches Him off guard. He knows *everything* you are going to go through. He
knows the solution and outcome of every situation. He has already made a way.
Depend on God during times of trouble so He can comfort you. Do not let
your circumstances get the best of you because when you do, you can become
blindsided and vulnerable to the tricks of the enemy. Put your trust in the One
who can bring you out. Put on the full armor of God and fight back. God not only
comforts you, but He equips you with everything you need to overcome. Use the
power and authority God has given you. Walk in victory because the enemy is
already defeated. You have no choice but to win! Your truth and your testimony
will encourage and comfort others through their times of trouble.

REFLECTION

Do you feel weighed down by your burdens? Is your baggage too heavy for you to carry? Cast [release] your burdens on the Lord. He wants to shower you with comfort. Release everything that is bothering you, weighing you down, or overwhelming you. Let there be an exchange – your burdens for His comfort. Once you lay it down, don't pick it back up. As you go through this week, be attentive to the ways God comforts you and write it down so when you are feeling discouraged or weighed down you can look back on it. You can encourage yourself knowing that if God did it before, He will do it again. Also, be attentive to opportunities God may give you to comfort others as well and write it down.

Release:

_____

_____

_____

_____

_____

_____

_____

Ways God comforted you:

_____

_____

_____

_____

_____

_____

_____

Ways you comforted others:

_____

_____

_____

_____

_____

_____

_____

Week 51

SMALL BEGINNINGS

Do not despise these small beginnings, for the Lord rejoices to see the work begin, to see the plumb line in Zerubbbabel's hand." (The seven lamps represent the eyes of the Lord that search all around the world.)
~~Zechariah 4:10 NLT~~

Walking in purpose is not always easy. You may run into roadblocks. You may not have the financial means or resources or the right connections. Maybe you don't feel supported by those close to you. But one thing for sure – God told you to do something. Maybe He told you to write a book, start a business, relocate, host a conference, submit a proposal, or apply for a particular job.

You want to be obedient, so you step out on faith. You begin to fast and pray over the thing God told you to do. You begin to plan and put in the work, and then boom! You're faced with an obstacle, the enemy comes after your mind, or you undergo warfare. You start to question whether you heard God correctly. You're on the brink of giving up. You're trying to be obedient but you wonder if it's worth it. Guess who else probably felt that way? Noah when he was building the ark, Mary when she became the target of the town's gossip for being pregnant with Jesus, Esther when she found out Haman was trying to destroy all the Jews, and Job when he lost everything. These people all have something in common. They all took a leap of faith. God changed their situation. They completed their purpose and literally changed the world. Despite the challenges and hardships they faced, their press impacted the lives of so many people, and so will you.

The Lord rejoiced when He saw you take that first leap of faith and began to put in the work. He never said it was going to be easy, but it's up to you to push through the challenges. You've already accomplished the most difficult part, and that was giving God your yes and getting started. Do not despise your small beginnings. The finish line may seem so far away, but every step you take brings you one step closer to the finish line. This journey takes faith and trust in God. You are not alone. God will connect you to the right people and provide you with everything you need to do what He told you to do. Remember, it's not about you, but about every person that is connected to your purpose. God wants to use you to impact your family, your job, your community, your church, your state or even the nations. You do not know the lives that will be changed by your obedience. You are meant to leave a mark on this earth that will leave a legacy far after you're gone. You are enough and more than capable of doing all that God called you to do.

REFLECTION

This week's declaration:
I have a purpose and I am purpose-driven. I will be all that God called me to be. I will have a productive day. God will supply all my needs according to His riches in glory. I will overcome every roadblock, obstacle, and hardship. I cast down false imagination and every lie from the enemy. I walk by faith and not by sight. God is able to do exceedingly abundantly above all that I ask or think according to the power that works in me. God who has begun a good work in me will complete it until the day of Jesus Christ. I am more than able to carry out His purpose for my life.

Antoine de Saint-Exupéry said, "a goal without a plan is just a wish." God is a very strategic God, and though He may have told you to do something, it is important that you ask Him for wisdom, discernment, and direction. You cannot expect God to drop everything in your lap. You have to put in the work too. He cares about every detail of your life and He is there to guide you through the process. Maybe the vision seems too big and starting is overwhelming. Ask yourself questions such as, "what resources do I need?" or "are there grants available for what I want to do?" or "which one of my friends, family members, coworkers, church family could I ask for help based on their gifts and talents?" Take baby steps. Write the vision and make it plain and go forth.

_____

_____

_____

_____

_____

_____

_____

_____

_____

_____

_____

_____

_____

_____

Week 52

INTIMACY WITH THE FATHER

He sent an angel to present this revelation to his servant John,
who faithfully reported everything he saw. This is his report
of the word of God and the testimony of Jesus Christ.
~~Revelation 1:1-2 NLT~~

God found John faithful enough to share the events that took place in the book of Revelation. God needed someone He could trust who would report everything He wanted to reveal. John's faithfulness was rooted in his relationship with the Father. Trust is built with intimacy and intimacy is built by spending time and getting to know someone. John had proven his trust and commitment to God – not because he wanted to gain something in return, but because of his love for the Father.

John was part of Jesus' inner circle. Jesus took Peter, James, and John on a high mountain where Jesus showed them his transfiguration. John was also referred to as the one whom Jesus loved. Lastly, when Jesus was being crucified, He trusted John with the responsibility of taking care of His mother. Jesus loved all His disciples, but John was the one who walked with Jesus on a more intimate level.

Your best friend is the one you are going to choose to be your maid of honor or best man. Your best friend is the one you are going to trust to be your child's godparent. This is the person that has stood the test of time. This the person you can share your secrets with. This is your confidant – the one you can be completely vulnerable and honest with. That was Jesus' relationship with John.

Before you become a friend of God, you have to be postured as a son/daughter. It is no different than a parent/child relationship. As a parent, you have to teach your child respect, enforce disciplinary actions, invest in their future, and have open communication. As the child grows up, the dynamics of the relationship change. The title of mom or dad does not change, but a level of friendship has developed.

That is how God wants to be with you. Even as a friend of God, you will always be a son/daughter first. Regardless of where you are in your relationship with God, He wants you to encounter Him, and He wants to share His heart with you. If you want to grow in this area, get in your secret place, spend time in the Word of God, develop your prayer life, and become disciplined as a listener of God's voice. In a busy world, we have not mastered the art of patience or trained ourselves to sit in silence for a long period of time. Silence can be uncomfortable, but it's in the quiet place where you can hear God's still small voice the loudest.

REFLECTION

Examine and evaluate your relationship with God. Maybe you have a strong relationship with God or maybe it's not where you want it to be. It is my prayer that by the end of these 52 weeks, you have come into the fullness of your identity as a son or daughter, and have found yourself in terms of your relationship with God. It is my prayer that your relationship with God has grown deeper and more intimate. After examining your relationship, write down where you want your relationship to be in the next 3-6 months. Write down your strengths and weaknesses in your relationship with God. Write down areas of improvement and things you can do to develop that relationship.

Additional Lined Pages

Week 1

Week 2

Week 3

Week 4

Week 5

Week 6

Week 7

Week 8

Week 9

Week 10

Week 11

Week 12

Week 13

Week 14

Week 15

Week 16

Week 17

Week 18

Week 19

Week 20

Week 21

Week 22

Week 23

Week 24

Week 25

Week 26

Week 27

Week 28

Week 29

Week 30

Week 31

Week 32

Week 34

Week 35

Week 36

Week 37

Week 38

Week 39

Week 42

Week 44

Week 45

Week 46

Week 47

Week 48

Week 49

Week 50

Week 51

Week 52

NOTES

Week 5
Receiving Power
1   "G1411 - dynamis - Strong's Greek Lexicon (kjv)." Blue Letter Bible. Web. 6 Feb, 2019. https://www.blueletterbible.org/lexicon/g1411/kjv/tr/0-1/.

Week 6
God is Able
2   "G1754 - energeō - Strong's Greek Lexicon (kjv)." Blue Letter Bible. Web. 7 Feb, 2019. https://www.blueletterbible.org/lexicon/g1754/kjv/tr/0-1/.

Week 10
God is Seeking
3   "H1875 - dāraš - Strong's Hebrew Lexicon (kjv)." Blue Letter Bible. Web. 11 Feb, 2019. https://www.blueletterbible.org/lexicon/h1875/kjv/wlc/0-1/.

Week 12
Putting in the Work
4   "G4735 - stephanos - Strong's Greek Lexicon (kjv)." Blue Letter Bible. Web. 8 Feb, 2019. https://www.blueletterbible.org/lexicon/g4735/kjv/tr/0-1/

Week 14
True Worship
5   "G4352 - proskyneō - Strong's Greek Lexicon (kjv)." Blue Letter Bible. Web. 8 Feb, 2019. https://www.blueletterbible.org/lexicon/g4352/kjv/tr/0-1/

Week 33
Here I Am!
6   Miller, Larry. Hineni. Weekly Standard, 2007. Accessed 8 Feb, 2019. https://www.washingtonexaminer.com/weekly-standard/hineni

Week 44
Made Strong in Weakness
7   "G5484 – charis - Strong's Greek Lexicon (kjv)." Blue Letter Bible. Web. 3 June, 2021. https://www.blueletterbible.org/lexicon/g5484/kjv/tr/0-1/

ABOUT THE AUTHOR

Alesha Dobos was born in Ohio and raised in Maryland, where she currently resides. She has bachelor's degree in Human Relations and is currently pursuing her master's in Psychology.

Alesha was raised in the church but didn't fully grasp what her relationship with God could be. At a very young age, she was always interested in knowing the God she read about in the Bible. She remembers reading about God speaking to people, people prophesying, being raised from the dead, being healed, and demons being casted out – none of what she saw in the church. As a young child, she would often question, "God, if You are the same yesterday, today, and forever, then I know You can do what You did in the Bible today. How do people hear from You? What does Your voice sound like? I want to have dreams and visions. I want to heal people. I want an encounter with You. Why don't we see more prophecy, healings, miracles, and deliverance in church? Where is the God of the Bible?" Despite all of her questions, Alesha always knew God was with her.

It wasn't until college that Alesha realized that church and the pursuit of intimacy with God wasn't just for adults. One evening, she went to a Bible study where she saw young adults praying in tongues and studying Greek and Hebrew to better understand the original translation and meaning of the Bible. Conviction set in and on her way back to her dorm room, she rededicated her life to Christ. She wanted relationship and intimacy with the Father. However, she felt a void she didn't understand. Despite her desperation, she felt there was distance between her and God, which resulted in ups and downs in her relationship with the Father.

However, in 2019, Alesha walked into her current church, The Father's House of Baltimore. Alesha was broken, struggling in every area of her life, wasn't walking in purpose, and was on the verge of giving up. For the first time in church, she experienced the God of the Bible that she read about so many times since her youth. It was here that she received true deliverance, discovered God as her Father, came into her identity as a daughter, became whole, was hopeful about her future, and went on a journey to pursue purpose.

It has taken Alesha three years to birth Walk into Purpose. Looking back, she realizes all of the hardships and challenges of writing this book was for a greater purpose. She could not give birth to rejection, comparison, pride, insecurity, and fear, and bleed on her readers. She needed to heal, be secure in her identity as a daughter, and become whole before she could truly walk in purpose. Years of walking aimlessly through life has given her the passion to see others free and walking in purpose as well.

Printed in the United States
by Baker & Taylor Publisher Services